In this inspirational book, acclaimed weaver and textile artist Rachna Garodia reveals the secrets of her weaving practice. Well known for her richly textured, evocative woven pieces, often incorporating flowers and foliage, recycled fabrics and found objects, here she explores ways of finding ideas, collecting materials, planning a design, and executing her weaves, using a wide range of techniques from simple weaving on paper to working on large floor-based looms.

In chapters arranged around the concept of contemplative, mindful walks, Rachna takes you through several key sources of inspiration and ways of working. In **Woodland Walk** she explores gathering and incorporating materials from nature such as leaves, grasses, flowers, bark and seed pods, while in **River Walk** she discusses the profound influence of flowing water on her work. **Walk Through the Seasons** explains how the creative mind can take inspiration from every season to create stunning pieces of work, and **Daily Commute** introduces the notion of meditative walking, and weaving with photographs to create quirky, disjointed images. **A Walk Down Memory Lan**e shows how to draw deep on your memories and use special objects and fabrics to create work that is meaningful to you, and finally **Walk With a Poem in Your Heart** showcases woven pieces inspired by great literature, some using books themselves.

Gorgeously illustrated with work from the author and other artists from around the world, this book is an engaging and beautiful introduction to the joys of weaving, both for established textile artists and for those coming to the craft for the first time.

CONTEMPORARY WEAVING IN MIXED MEDIA

Low Tide (detail). Handwoven, incorporating driftwood and twigs found on a river walk.

CONTEMPORARY WEAVING IN MIXED MEDIA

RACHNA GARODIA

BATSFORD

Lavender Fields, 42 × 52cm (16½ × 20½in), framed. Handwoven with silk, wool, cotton, leather, paper and dried lavender.

First published in the United Kingdom in 2022 by

B. T. Batsford Ltd
43 Great Ormond Street
London
WC1N 3HZ

An imprint of B. T. Batsford Holdings Limited

ISBN 978 1 84994 765 7

A CIP catalogue record for this book is available from the British Library.

10 9 8 7 6 5 4 3 2 1

Reproduction by Rival Colour Ltd, UK
Printed and bound by Toppan Leefung Printing Ltd, China

CONTENTS

INTRODUCTION

Weaving is a craft I have trained in, practised, honed and admired for over half my life. I am still learning and refining my own work as I continue to grow as an artist and develop my practice. This book is not a 'learn how to weave' book; rather, it is an exploration of my own textile practice that is intended to provide inspiration. I focus on my inspirations for these works, revealing how the natural world is my muse, accomplice and mentor.

Walking – through nature especially – is an integral part of my creative practice. I do my best thinking when out on foot and find it a natural, effective way to distil mindfulness into spontaneous ideas. The poet Wallace Stevens sums it up well:

**'In my room, the world is beyond my understanding
But when I walk I see it consists of three or four hills and a cloud.'**

Each chapter is a visual diary of my creative process: gathering and preparing materials; drawing; photographing; and making mood boards. This ultimately leads to pieces of textile art created with various loom and non-loom techniques, which I will share.

In some chapters, I have included a textile to examine, to consider how it has influenced not only me but the wider textile world. I find that we are always shaped by what is around us as well as what came before us. It is thus important to look closely at ancient weaving, for instance, to really appreciate the value of a high-quality piece of work and to understand the techniques, artistry and craftsmanship that went into it. Our creative forces today are built out of the past, with a contemporary approach and ideas.

With this book, I am pleased to share my inspirations, my process and my work. I hope my story will spark ideas and inspire and encourage you to go on your own journey, whether you are a beginner or a more experienced weaver. Learn the language of your local wild flowers, birds and trees; surround yourself with the riches nature so generously bestows on us.

Landscape, handwoven screen, 71 × 97cm (28 × 38in), framed. Cotton, jute, rayon, sisal on a nylon monofilament warp incorporating dried wheat pods.

Woodland Walk, 98 × 103cm (38½ × 40½in), displayed on the loom. Handwoven, incorporating willow, cinnamon and bark with wool, linen and cotton yarns.

①

WOODLAND WALK

'In every walk with nature, one receives far more than he seeks.'

John Muir

My work is informed by observing the natural world: it is constantly changing, yet still. My initial impetus to create has always come from nature, and I often go on long walks to spark my creative process. Being among trees – gathering, collecting and pocketing fallen leaves, twigs, seed pods and bark – helps create a refuge from the chaos of the outside world. The internal quietness I experience when among trees is really important for me to focus on that 'nameless something' bursting to be formed.

When I say 'woodland', I do not necessarily mean a forest – or, indeed, that you have to have a studio in the woods. I have always lived in cities and my 'woodland' has always been the closest green patch I can find, whether that is my garden, the trees along the pavements around my house, or Richmond Park, which is close to my current studio.

In 2006, when I moved from Mumbai to London, I was amazed to find such a different world of flora and fauna. I fell in love with the little flowers bursting on pavements and brick walls. Dandelions, daisies, buttercups and herb Robert were my first friends in England. Armed with a wild flower and tree spotting guide, I befriended London plane, oak, poplar, magnolia and gingko. Knowing these trees around the neighbourhood made me feel happier and more at home.

10

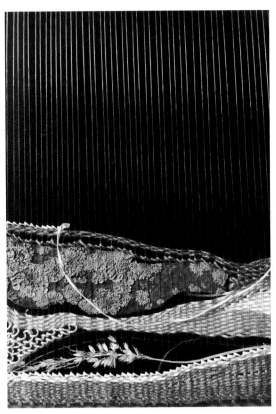

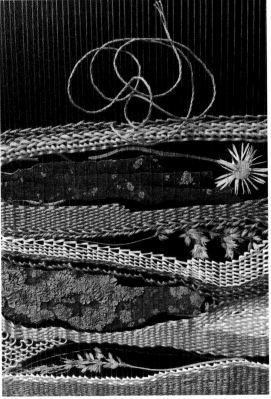

Try to gather inspiration from the environment around you, however urban or rural it is. A garden patch, an overgrown roundabout, a few flowerpots, or a sea front, rocky hillside, wild moor or field of rapeseed – all of these environments, tiny or vast, can brim with life and beauty. Tune in to your surroundings: be mindful and use your imagination.

Above: Gathered materials prepared and matched with yarns. Above right and left: weaving in progress in different stages incorporating the found materials.

INSPIRATION
FROM NATURE

Sometimes a single leaf can move me so much with its beauty – a continuous lesson in colour blending – that I'm filled with a sense of abundant possibilities and can't wait to get working in the studio. All of my collected objects, such as leaves, twigs, seed pods, cones and acorns, are added to the curiosity table in my studio. Found objects placed together in a meaningful arrangement take on a collective significance, expressing the wideness and wonder of this world, and helping my imagination and creativity to flow.

It is important for me to photograph, draw and sometimes print my findings, as these found objects rapidly change colour and texture. Although I love to observe and record these changes, sometimes I just want to preserve the memory of a leaf exactly as I found it, and a photo or a sketch is the best way to do this.

My ever-growing collection of pressed flowers and leaves is like a bank of inspiration, perfect for when seasons turn and I need a feel of spring in winter to proceed on a project. I use various types of traditional flower presses for pressing leaves and flowers. A DIY version – two pieces of hardboard with layers of leaves between blotting paper with weights on top – works fine too.

Bark is fascinating as well. Apart from helping one to identify tree types, especially deciduous trees in winter, the distinct textures are absorbing: the wispy, ribbon-like strips of the silver birch, for example; the deep ridges and cracks of the English oak, or the smooth bark of the beech tree with 'eyes' that seem to follow you. Pine bark flakes off in plates, and the bark of London planes has beautiful camouflage patterns, made more attractive when wet with rain. I especially love lichens and moss on bark. I have a large collection of plane tree bark covered in vivid lichens.

12

Inspiration table showing a collection of sourced
and gathered materials from several walks.

Journal incorporating birch bark collected on a walk as inspiration to develop
a natural colour palette for future weaves.

Windy days are particularly good for collecting pieces of bark. The
top rule of collecting is to pick what's on the ground, never directly from
the trees, as that would harm them. After cleaning the bark, I usually
press it down with a heavy weight to flatten it as much as possible,
especially if I want to incorporate it in my weaves. If the pieces are too
dry and curled up, I spray them lightly with water to make them supple,
then straighten them out gently before pressing.

Seed pods are a personal favourite. Nature's ingenious packaging
keeps the seeds safe from predators and allows them to travel easily on
the breeze to pollinate far and wide. The raw beauty of these marvels
never ceases to amaze and inspire me. I don't think I could ever see
enough magnolia pods, with their bright seeds popping out slowly
against the grey London sky, while the brown seed pods from locust
trees make a frequent appearance in my weaves. I gently open these
papery pods to reveal the seeds nestling within the shiny interior, which
acts as a beautiful contrast when paired with natural yarns such as
cotton, linen and wool.

Detail of a weave using seed pods, birch bark and other natural materials in combination with wool, cotton, rayon and linen yarns.

GATHERING MATERIALS

A dry day is best for gathering, preparing and storing these natural materials, preferably in late afternoon after the dew has dried and before the evening damp sets in. Sometimes I carry a plastic bag or box with me so the more delicate flowers such as buttercups and daisies don't get crushed under a piece of bark or a pod.

Gathering does not have to be a summer pastime; you can find materials all year round. I find it interesting to observe the secrets of the natural world, the interplay between plants and their environment, where they grow and how they reproduce, to see how they change through the seasons. To obtain a broader range of colour to work with, experiment with gathering grasses when they are both green and brown.

The fresh and delicate flowers and leaves that I collect are usually pressed in a flower press or between sheets of blotting paper under a weight. Avoid using kitchen towels, as the textured surface leaves an imprint. I ended up with a whole batch of polka-dotted daisies once!

Dried foliage collection ready for weaving.

Smaller flower presses with a few of my favourite seasonal delights.

I air dry the rest of my gathered materials in a warm, dry and well-ventilated area. Dust, soot, grease and light can prevent you from getting the best results. There are various chemicals that speed up the drying process, but I prefer to dry my materials naturally, avoiding unnecessary chemical additives.

Each plant has a different drying time, but most usually dry after three to five weeks. I like to coat them with matt varnish to preserve them longer. My advice is to experiment and learn more by trying different methods, and not limiting yourself to familiar plants and seasons. For instance, I am often tempted to buy bunches of dried foliage sold at florists if they are new and unfamiliar varieties to me, and types I do not have access to in my regular foraging.

CHOOSING A LOOM

Weaving can be as high-tech or as low-tech as you want it to be. You can weave the most beautiful pieces on a basic frame; the difference is the amount of time taken and the complexity and sophistication of your design.

Personally, for smaller pieces, I like weaving on small wooden frames that are quick to set up; I can experiment with materials and colours more quickly and set up the bigger loom once I have an idea of what I want to weave. These weaving frames can even be made out of mount boards with notches for warp yarns.

When choosing a frame for small-size weaving, I tend to go for ones with strong corners that do not warp with the tight tension of yarns. For larger pieces, I prefer my table loom or the floor loom.

I list books, websites and blogs that offer in-depth information on weaving tools and techniques in the resources section on page 126.

18

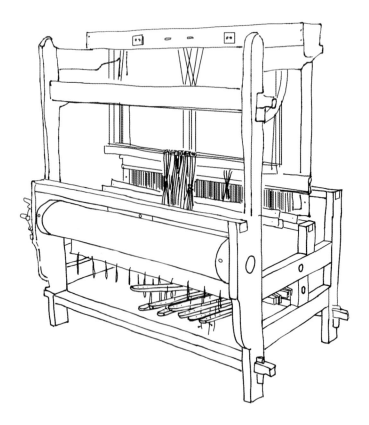

1.

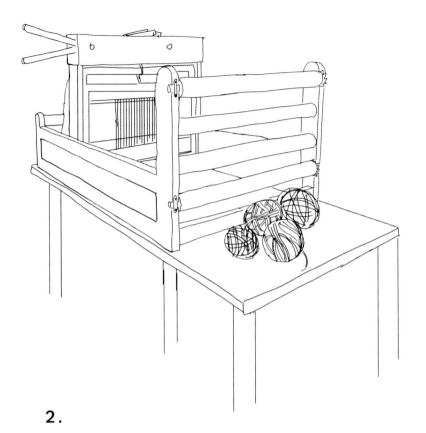

1. Handbuilt four-shaft countermarch floor loom, single beam, Texsolv heddles.

2. Handbuilt table loom, showing four shafts here but with a capacity to accommodate 12 shafts, double beam, metal heddles.

3. Self-made high warp pipe loom with handmade continuous cotton heddles for lifting alternate warp.

4. Frame loom with reinforced corners for strength and durability so that when stretching warp in high tension any distortion of the frame can be avoided.

2.

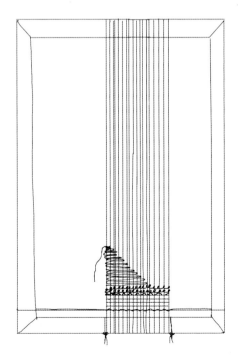

3.

4.

THE CREATIVE PROCESS

Once I have prepared the natural materials that I intend to use in a piece, I do a quick sketch of the kind of shapes I want to create on the loom and where I will place the intended materials. Then comes the task of deciding on the colours and type of warp and weft yarns. The warp is usually nylon monofilament, natural or white cotton or linen. For the weft, I like to use a combination of natural yarns such as wool, jute, cotton, nettle, hemp, raffia, paper and waste fabric strips.

All yarns have their own unique feel and texture; using a combination of these together in one woven piece adds interest to the finished surface.

Selecting the material palette is the most important step in my design process. I like to live with my colour and material choices for a day or two before I am convinced about the selection. This step becomes easier with more practice; over time, selection becomes second nature.

Then comes a period of intense concentration during which I start the process of warping and setting up the loom, while stealing glances at my

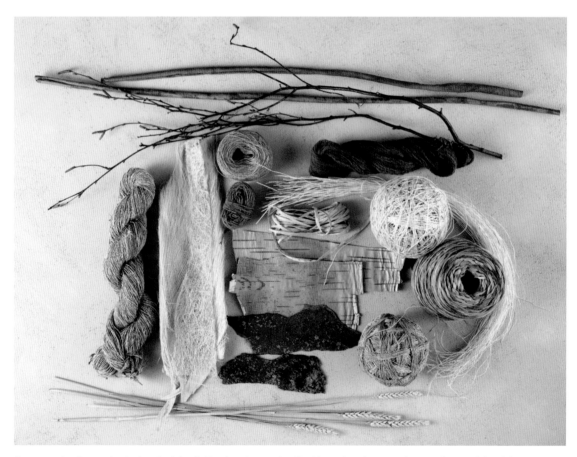

An example of my selected material palette showing a mix of gathered and sourced natural materials with a combination of yarns, ready to weave.

Journals with mood, colour and material inspiration and weave planning.

combination of yarns and visualizing the final piece. Once satisfied with my choice, I begin to weave. The line drawing, which I stick on the side of the loom, acts as a guide, and all my intended materials are laid out next to the loom on boards. Nothing stops me from adding an accent colour or deleting a colour altogether once the weaving begins, but I rarely need to.

There are days when things do not go as planned and some colours do not sit together as well as I expected, but I'm always grateful that I have the option to go back, unweave an area I'm not happy with, and replace it with another colour, thickness or pattern.

Graham Wallas, social psychologist and co-founder of the London School of Economics, came up with a ground-breaking four-stage model of the creative process, detailed in his 1926 book *The Art of Thought*. This explains where ideas come from and how we coax them into manifestation. I find the model very helpful to my own creative process and follow it for even the smallest of my weaves.

Wallas's four stages are:

Preparation Understanding the work in hand, accumulating resources and investigating in all directions.
Incubation A period of unconscious processing where long walks are most beneficial.
Illumination The final flash, which is the culmination of a successful train of association.
Verification Conscious work that follows the inspiration, that demands immense attention and discipline in execution.

The stages constantly overlap as I work on various projects and explore new ideas. I have shared studios with many creatives in the last few years and have observed that the period of 'incubation' is often mistaken for 'procrastination'. It is thus important to realize the importance of incubation, where you consciously let go of the work at hand and let the subconscious take over. When creatives 'dream up' a new piece of work, it is usually the result of a lot of conscious and subconscious energy spent on research that leads to the 'illuminating' idea. However, you have to be aware when it's time to stop thinking and start putting those ideas into action.

I sometimes weave small personal pieces to memorialize a special day or event. For me, most of these unforgettable moments tend to be outdoors, spent with people I love. *Kite Flying Day* and *Lavender Fields* are two such pieces; they hold the spirit of the day and moment perfectly, preserving it better than any photograph could. Perhaps these weaves are so special because they are woven with little treasures that grew on the ground we walked on, preserving all the gaiety and energy of the day, charging these memories with life.

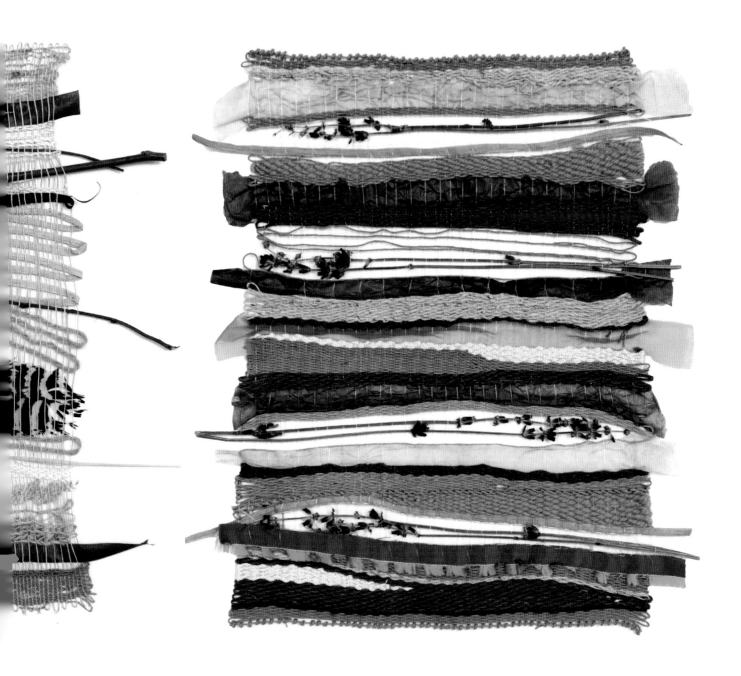

Above left: *Kite Flying Day.* Wool, cotton, jute, raffia with twigs, feather, grass on a nettle warp.

Above: *Lavender Fields.* Silk, wool, cotton, leather, paper with dried lavender on a nylon monofilament warp.

WORKING WITH FEATHERS

Birds have always been a significant source of inspiration during my walks. The immeasurable joy I find in a quick flash of blue or green when a jay or a woodpecker flies past is hard to express in words; it finds a voice in my weaves in the form of a feather woven in, capturing the magic of flight and open skies. Any feather I chance upon, if it's not too wet or muddy, finds a way into my studio jar as inspiration and material for future use.

Feathers – these soft, delicate, surprisingly durable, colourful objects, imbued with spiritual energy and supernatural force – have been used for thousands of years across cultures for adornment and decoration.

I find Peruvian featherworks one of the most intriguing types of textiles; used for garments, headdresses, personal ornaments and ritual objects, the feathers signify high social standing because of their rarity and brilliant colours. I am also attracted to the immense creativity, dexterity and artistic sensitivity of the craftspeople who made them. Feathers were tied to strings either individually or in groups. They were then laid onto the woven fabrics row by row, starting at the bottom and moving upwards, and stitched into place. The closer they are knotted, the plusher the fabric.

Living and working in West London, I'm really lucky to have access to parks and gardens to stay inspired and keep my creativity flowing. A sense of belonging also comes from knowing what grows around me and paying attention to the constantly

Collected feathers from various walks in London are strung together.

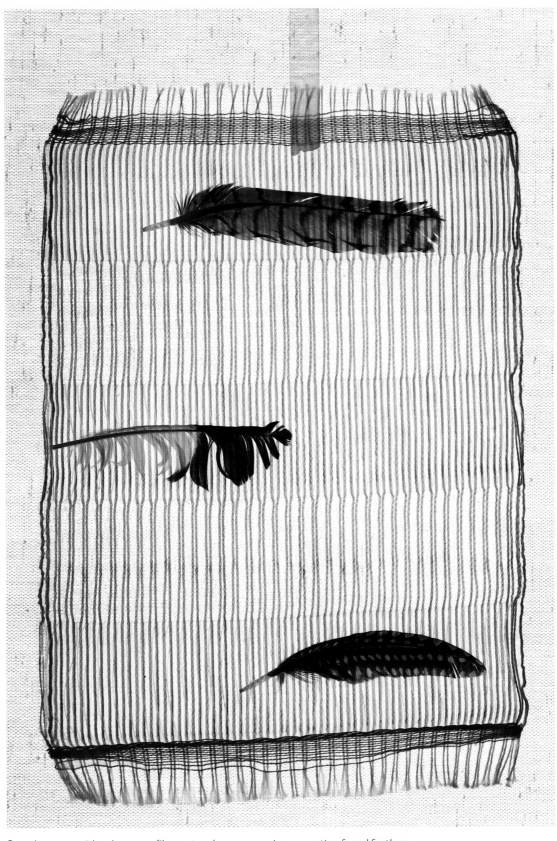

Sample woven with nylon monofilament and rayon warp incorporating found feathers.

Huari Feather mini tunic, c. 800 AD, Huari culture, feathers and camelid fibres,
25 × 32 cm (9¾ × 12½in). Courtesy Paul Hughes Fine Arts.

ADDING FEATHERS
AND FOLIAGE

The techniques employed in creating Peruvian
feathered textiles were ingenious and can be
translated into contemporary weaving using
materials such as leaves, quills and paper.

A simple twining technique can be used to string
together feathers or leaves (see illustration above).

Inspired by my long walks, *Richmond Park*, 58 × 80cm (22¾ × 31½in), is woven with nettle, cotton, jute, linen, raffia, wheat pods and maple keys on a cotton warp.

evolving and changing forms. Woodland walks, any time from dawn to dusk, whether a two-hour ramble or a 15-minute commune with the outside world, ground me as well as giving me a sense of connection with the wider world. John Muir sums it up:

> 'This grand show is eternal
> It is always sunrise somewhere;
> The dew is never dried all at once;
> A shower is forever falling; vapour is ever rising.
> Eternal sunrise, eternal dawn and gloaming,
> on sea and continents and islands,
> Each in its turn, as the round earth rolls.'

Riverwash, 98 × 98cm (38½ × 38½in), framed. Handwoven with jute, raffia, silk, linen and cotton yarn on a nylon monofilament warp.

RIVER WALK

'Rivers know this: there is no hurry. We shall get there some day.'

A. A. Milne

Historically, we, as a people, have gone to the river with our joys as well as our sorrows, given them all to the river and felt lighter after. Rivers have been a site of reverence, ritual and celebration since ancient times. Many stories, poems and artworks have been dreamt up on a river's bridges, tunnels and along its banks. There are always elements of history, awe, magic and intrigue in the swirls of the river, and few are left untouched by its luminosity. I am no different; all my problems seem smaller and my jumbled thoughts get ironed out after a walk by a river.

I grew up in India and my school was very close to the bank of the River Ganga/Ganges. Ganga was revered but also feared; she is the holy mother, protector, giver of life but also the destroyer. We visited the banks during festivals and auspicious occasions with offerings and hopes of being blessed. Ganga was always sacred.

It was easy enough to befriend the River Thames when I moved to West London in 2006, not only because it was a short walk from our house but because I found myself fascinated by its tidal nature. After the full-flowing Ganga I was shocked when I saw the Thames at its lowest ebb, almost like a trickle. Could this really be a river? Coming across George Alexander's *Father Thames* sculpture at Hammersmith Town Hall added to the intrigue. This river was 'male', challenging my concept of a beautiful, feminine river that I had developed with the Ganga. I even have an auntie called Ganga.

Twice a day, the Thames in London swells with the tide, rising as much as 7m (23ft). As the water gradually recedes, it leaves behind 'treasures' in the form of broken pottery, old coins, buttons, clay pipes, rusted nails and more. These weathered fragments found along the river bed record the sun, rain, wind and cold in a unique language of discolouration, rust, tarnish, shrinking and cracking. Like many before me, I am fascinated by this tidal phenomenon and am pulled to the river, wanting to share my stories with it and create new ones, continuing a long tradition. Please note, though, that in London taking items from the river shore requires a permit.

Long walks by the river are an essential part of my life. The river has seen my children grow from toddlers to teens. When I weave a collection inspired by the river, it is the Thames physically but the Ganga spiritually. The Thames feels, in a way, like a bunch of threads flowing in harmony, weaving us together, combining our past and present, creating the most beautiful stories along its way in a delightful rhythmic motion.

30

A collection of gathered fragments from along the shore of the River Thames.

INSPIRATION FROM THE RIVER

Standing in front of the River Thames, I watch the water flow, feel the cold, rippling, reflecting surface, as water moves around the stones, changing its dull, grey surface to sparkling ochre and black, shimmering and brimming with life. The charm with which the sun, the moon and the twilight play on the face of the river fills me with ceaseless wonder. Observing the rippling, reflecting river, I get sucked into its rhythm. I see the sky, the clouds, the birds, trees and – is that me, staring back? We are all one, flowing along; we are the river.

Journal incorporating sketches, photos and collected shells and pebbles from a river walk.

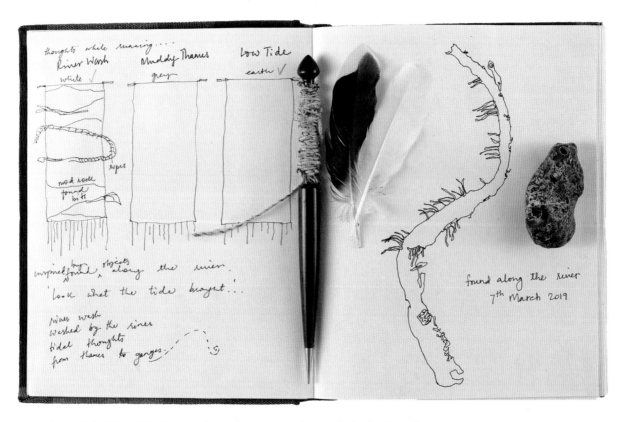

Journal with ideas jotted down after reflecting upon long walks by the River Thames.

Back in the studio, I meditate on my walk. I reflect on my finds: driftwood, broken tiles, a shell, rusted metals, beautiful stones, some rounded and smooth, some sharp. Touching each of them, holding them, I feel the river flowing through me. It is with these thoughts that I imagine, interpret and create my weaves.

The quickest way to start a new weaving project is to list words that come to mind when I think of my river walks. I also make a few notes and jot down observations. Building on a few recurring words and thoughts I then move ahead, making quick line drawings and sketches. I print out the photos that I took on my walks to include in my journal – visual fodder for new ideas.

Journal with a list of reflective words that help in generating new ideas for weaves.

While I'm working, I sometimes listen to podcasts and read writings about the river to further inspire me. My key motivation is to expand my weaving boundaries and to create using minimal tools, being simple in my approach, almost with a beginner's mind. Then, while preparing the materials I gathered, some as inspiration and some to actually incorporate into the weaves, I like to pore over ancient textiles for fresh ideas. Where techniques are concerned, there are times when I feel there is nothing that has not been tried before. But then I tune into my inner voice and my deep compulsion to create, to give my emotions and my experiences a tangible form through weaves created by my own two hands.

WEAVING ON PAPER

I love weaving on paper – it is a fun way to execute smaller weaves. Here I share my method and on the following pages you can see some examples.

• Take some thick paper; here I used 350gsm. On the reverse side, draw an outline of the weave's shape with a pencil.

• Mark tiny prick points on opposite ends all along the shape with a fine needle. If the holes are too close together, there is a chance of tearing; if they are too far apart the weave will be an open one. You want to find the right balance.

• Thread a needle with the warp yarn and leave a long tail at the back. Make no knots. Insert through the last hole from the back, then come up to the front and then the hole at the opposite end. Repeat.

I prefer the warping to be continuous and taut; you can adjust the tension by gently pulling at the tail end.

Once the threads are taut, you can knot the ends at the back, and start to weave.

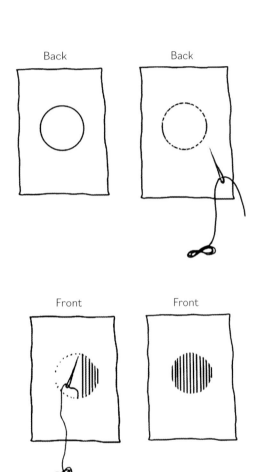

Back Back

Front Front

RIVER HAIKU

River Haiku, a collection of small weaves on paper, is an ode to the grace, beauty and poetry of the majestic River Thames. In this collection, I combined various natural yarns with objects found while mudlarking; the weaving was done on paper.

River Haiku, 23 × 30.5cm (9 × 12in) each. Eight in the collection, six shown here. A combination of wool, silk, linen, cotton and paper yarn with ceramic fragments from the river on a nylon monofilament warp.

River Haiku (detail). Handwoven on Khadi paper with wool, cotton and linen yarns incorporating a found ceramic fragment from a river walk.

HIGH TIDE AND LOW TIDE

River walks are a need, like nourishment for the soul, for my art to exist. The river flowing offers a quiet lesson on time, change and growth. The relentlessness of the tide, the daily up and down, is akin to thoughts that persist, that come and go. The natural regeneration and degeneration, the growth and decay, the daily rhythms. The low tide always makes me aware that the river is not just a river of water, but of rocks and stones, creatures and plants, history and amnesia, songs and stories. These thoughts led to the *High Tide* and *Low Tide* weaves.

Right: *High Tide*, 50 × 180cm (19¾ × 71in). Handwoven with paper, plastic, cotton, silk and linen yarns with found and treated objects from the river on a cotton warp.
Far right: *Low Tide*, 50 × 180cm (19¾ × 71in). Handwoven with jute, linen, cotton and silk yarns incorporating river finds on a cotton warp.

MUDDY THAMES

Being close to the river daily makes you more aware of its beauty but also acquaints you with the ecosystem's fragility. We are all connected – to the land, water and to each other – but the amount of waste and plastics that end up on the banks revealed by the low tide is alarming. It makes me question how we live and how far removed we are from the land that feeds us. My piece *Muddy Thames* was born from these questions.

I have dwelt on the repetitive and meditative aspect of a walk by the river with *Muddy Thames*, celebrating the stillness, grace and wisdom in this ancient waterway. My handwoven piece explores the feeling of solitude and kinship I find in the cyclical nature of high and low tides. Through this piece, I also lament the plastic polluting our water, especially the wet wipes, face masks, earbuds and other single-use plastics.

I used bin liner strips together with foraged bits collected during walks by the river. Young alders, buddleias and willows growing among the walls and arches along the banks, always waving trapped plastic bags, bottles and other pollutants, have inspired me, and served as a reminder to take responsibility for the way we live and to protect and care for what we love.

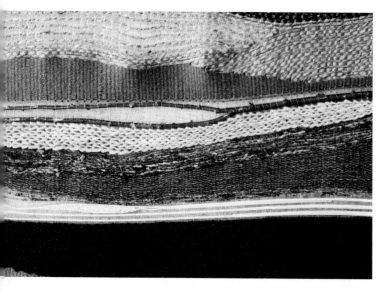

Muddy Thames. Detail of waste fabric tassels with driftwood and rusty metal finds from the river, and detail of weave showing a combination of soumak, leno and plain weaves (see page 124–125).

Muddy Thames, 93 × 84cm (36½ × 33in), handwoven with wool, cotton, plastic, paper, moss, driftwood and rusted metal found by the river.

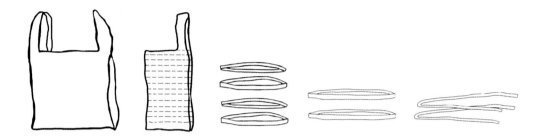

MAKING YARNS OUT OF PLASTIC BAGS

Joining looped plastic   Joining single strips

• Clean and wipe dry the plastic bag.

• Flatten and fold lengthwise.

• Cut into strips along the dotted lines shown above. If the plastic is very thin, keep the strips in loops, as shown right. If the plastic is thicker, cut loops from one end to make longer strips, then join by making a small cut at the end of two strips and making a knot as shown far right. This type of joining gives a little bump at the point of attachment.

MAKING PLASTIC CORDAGE

• Prepare lengths of waste plastics of the desired width. Start with two strips and fasten them to a fixed point, so that tension can be applied. Hold the strips, one in each hand.

• Twist the right-hand strip once or twice in a clockwise direction. Bring it over to the left-hand strip, keeping that as still as possible until you trap both between your left thumb and forefinger. Now twist the lower left-hand strip clockwise. Repeat.

• When only about 2.5cm (1in) of the strips is left, then, to join, lay a new strip over the right-hand strip and continue twisting them together into the cord. The tail can be cut later.

This method can also be used to make cordage out of newspaper, fabric and natural materials such as nettle, grass or raffia.

43

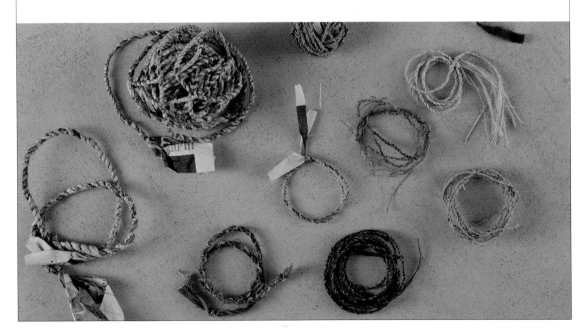

RIVER WEAVING WORKSHOP

Here I would like to mention an interesting collaboration I had with fellow artist and activist Camilla Brendon. As part of the Totally Thames Festival organized by Thames Festival Trust, an independent charity, Camilla and I ran a river weaving workshop, taking the participants on a walk by the river. We encouraged them to physically interact with the river and river bed and to gather items they found interesting while Camilla talked about the environmental issues faced by the Thames and other water systems. She focused on plastics and other pollutants, as well as the knock-on effects and connection with the wider ecosystem.

After the walk, everyone had a session on weaving, incorporating materials found by the river and using yarns made of plastic bags and waste textiles. It was very interesting to observe all the creative ways each participant interacted with the materials; the tiny weaves they completed were beautiful.

Small weaves by the participants at the River Weaving Workshop with yarns made of waste fabric and plastic, incorporating river finds like shells, keys, driftwood, etc.

44

45

Ganga and Thames, 45 × 115cm (17¾ × 45¼in). Handwoven with silk, linen, cotton, wool, shells and driftwood.

GANGA AND THAMES

For me, like most Hindus, the river completes the cycle of life. After death, the body is cremated, and the ash is preserved in clay pots to be immersed in rivers where water is flowing (usually Ganga). As the ashes are put into the holy water, the spirit is released from the body for its journey, shaped by the individual's good (or karma) during his or her life.

There is also an ancient Greek myth about throwing coins into the river as a payment for ferries that take the dead souls to the underworld. For me, dropping coins symbolizes good luck and fortune; when I chance upon a shiny coin in the river it always makes me happy. I take it as a sign of hope and the presence of something larger. Similarly, when I pick up a shell, a piece of wood or a stone from around any river, I feel it carries the energy and spirit of the departed, together with fragments of lost time. It is thus with a sort of reverence that I place them into my weaves.

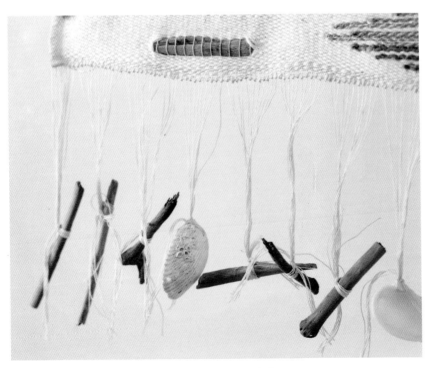

Ganga and Thames, detail of tassels created from shells and driftwood tied to the cotton warp.

DELUGE AND SCORCHED

Life flourishes and civilizations thrive alongside rivers, but while life-giving, rivers can also be unpredictable and snatch life in a single gulp. The contrast of a dried river bed with a flooded plain – both causing immense desolation – redoubles the mystery of this shifting, glinting, ever-flowing water. This combination of luminous moments and dark shadowy depths almost challenges the viewer to recognize and make meaning of the ebb and overflow, fertile and arid, life and death. I wove my pieces *Deluge* and *Scorched* with these thoughts, combining strips of old silk saris with jute and silk to depict the devastation caused by rivers' unpredictability.

All these years of living close to the River Thames and being lucky enough to have had temporary studios around the river has fed into my textile practice. Just like the Thames, I find myself sometimes still, sometimes raging. It soothes me that these feelings of high and low are natural and cyclical. Like the river, my job is to keep flowing and to do my work with joy and sparkle.

Above left: *Deluge*, 91 x 96cm (35¾ x 37¾in). Handwoven with strips of silk fabric, jute, wool and silk yarn.
Above right: *Scorched*, 87 x 92cm (34¼ x 36¼in). Handwoven with wool, cotton and silk yarn.

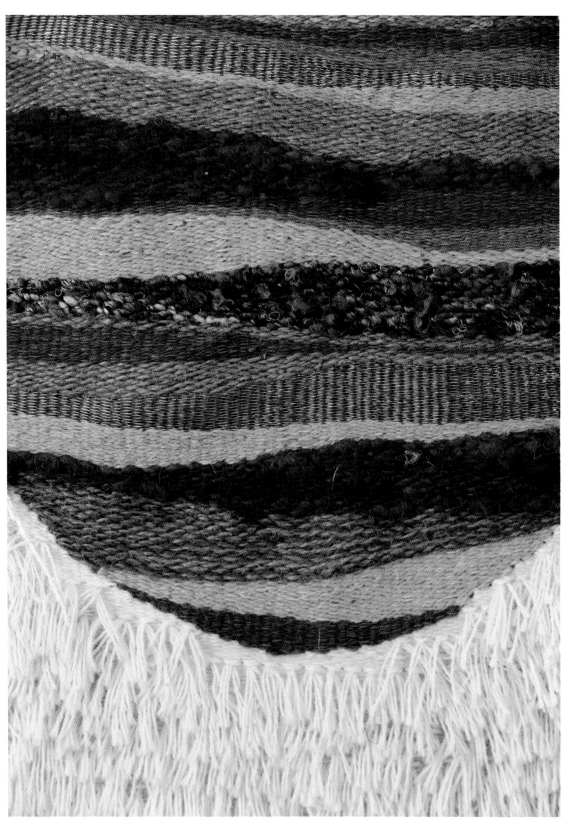

Scorched (detail). Handwoven using Turkish knot and plain weave, creating textures using weft yarn of varied thickness.

Petrichor, 23 × 130cm (9 × 51in). Dyed raffia, nettle and wool yarn.

3

WALK THROUGH THE SEASONS

'I think that to one in sympathy with nature
each season, in turn, seems the loveliest.'

Mark Twain

52

Observing the cycle of the seasons has been important to many people, both ancient and modern. The four seasons (spring, summer, autumn, winter) are often associated with a joyous, eternal cycle of life. In each there is a mood to inspire and reflect on. Spring, a time of regrowth and numerous possibilities; summer, long, endless days that invite relaxation; autumn, its lengthening of shadows and shorter days, brightened by the golden, yellow, red and orange hues of the changing leaves; winter, its bare landscape and crisp air, bathed in cold light.

I would like to add a fifth to this list. Growing up in India, monsoon was my favourite season, a short, much-awaited period providing respite from the heat. The sweet smell that accompanies the first rain as it falls on the parched earth marks its onset – the most memorable and magical moment.

When we were young, we took part in the children's ritual of getting wet in the first rains. We would jump, squeal, dance and delight in the heavens' opening; none of the grown-ups minded the mess and sneezes that followed – it was a moment of pure, abundant joy.

When rains make contact with dry, parched earth, there is a distinctive earthy odour that can be regarded as 'petrichor', the tenuous essence derived from rocks/stone ('petra'). I love the sound of this word and used it to name my monsoon-inspired panel.

Opposite: *Petrichor* (detail). Turkish knot at the edge with a mix of wool, cotton and linen yarns.

Right: *Petrichor* (detail). Woven on a linen warp with raffia, nettle and wool, this weave evokes all the memories and smells of a happy childhood dancing in the drenching rains.

53

INSPIRATION
FROM THE SEASONS

Recurring, cyclical, inevitable, the seasons turn, each with a distinct flavour, signifying the passage of time. This was especially apparent to me when I moved to England, where, unlike in India, each season is so distinct. I try to approach life with the understanding that each season, in its different ways, will teach us strength, endurance, growth, faith and trust, while also providing joy. The abundant summer, with its thriving flora and fauna, gives us warmth and hope after the cold, bleak, quieter winter months. There is a certain rhythm in the change and permanence of the seasonal cycle. We know when leaves start to fall that, while snow may come next, spring will eventually follow. It is this knowledge of spring and new life that allows us to enjoy autumn. Our delight at the changing seasons reflects an interesting paradox of human nature: we delight in the new as well as the old, and we yearn for change while simultaneously relishing in routine.

I'm no different. There are elements of each season that I love. In autumn, I delight in the colourful melody of the falling leaves, and my flower press is busiest from September through November. Winter, when the deciduous trees are bare of leaves, makes it easy to see the shapes of the trees, all the snaking branches and birds' nests that are hidden and protected by foliage in the warmer months. These trees, struck by winter sun against the backdrop of a bright blue sky, are sculptural and breathtaking in their stark beauty. Spring delights are many: the blossoms, bird song and flowers show me the promise of brighter and warmer days. My walks in spring are slower, with numerous stops to admire and get lost in the beauty of the fresh, green, sweet-smelling unfurling of life all around. During summer, I covet snoozes in the garden while the bees hum, drunk on the sweetness of lavender, and the swifts circle the sky.

Walking is the best way to 'see' the seasons unfold, how nature changes every day in response to the passing of the year. It helps foster a deep connection with the elemental world. The more we tune in, we more we can discover new insights about the transition of life. Woven on a hemp warp, *Hope* captures the unfolding of spring. The first few daffodils, snowdrops and fresh green promise brighter days to follow.

Opposite: *Hope*, approx. 60 × 100cm (23½ × 39¼in). Handwoven with nettle, raffia, cotton, linen, jute and Tencel yarn on a hemp warp.

HANDS

In India, one of the many games we played as children was palm reading. We grew up believing that all life has in store for you – your happiness, challenges, life partner, children – is 'written' on your hands. Every fold, mark, deep and faint line in your palm had a special meaning. We would pretend to read each other's destined future life, inventing great tales along the way.

Although this childhood game fizzled out and I never got into serious palmistry, I continue to believe that our life is predestined, but that we have total control over our response and attitude to all of life's offerings.

Hands is a collection of weaves that I created in response to celebrating time, change, seasons and our uniqueness as human beings. Each hand represents a season, woven with disparate finds; the various coloured yarns create diverse textures.

Above left: *Autumn Hand* on the loom. Above right: *Autumn Hand*. Handwoven with nettle, raffia, cotton, linen, jute and Tencel yarn on a hemp warp.

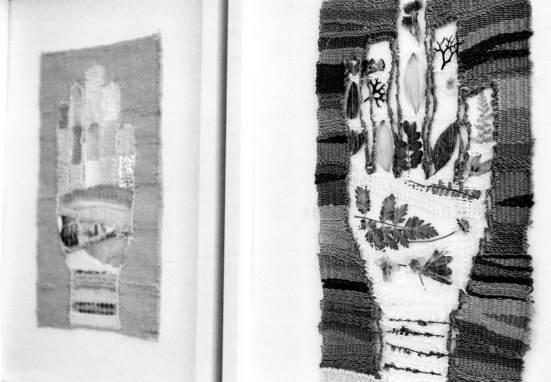

Top: *Winter Hand*, *Spring Hand* and *Autumn Hand*, 32 × 42cm (12½ × 16½in) each, framed. Above: *Winter Hand* and *Spring Hand* (details). Woven with linen, cotton and paper yarn with pressed flowers and leaves.

Seasonal delights on various walks: cherry blossoms; magnolia seed pods; photinia leaves in vivid colours; crunchy autumnal oak leaves.

Journal with mood and colour inspiration.

Each day reveals a subtle change, a little growth, a little decay and a little promise when we tune in to the natural world. My phone is replete with photos of these seasonal delights – the unfurling of leaves, how the soft protective wraps open, covering the tree to reveal soft new golden-green leaves, soon to be followed by flowers and fruits. I am grateful for witnessing such everyday magic in the cycle of nature, and to be able to pocket a few of these fallen treasures as a reminder of the world's wonders.

I am most drawn to the colours of changing seasons – the countless shades of greens blending with one another, the riot of English gardens in spring and summer. How can pink, yellow, orange, red, purple live in such perfect harmony? I feel that this vibrant colour palette gets passed on to the autumn leaves and I recall moments of ecstasy when observing beech leaves, in particular, carpeted under the tree, each leaf more beautiful than the last in its melody of green, brown and yellow.

BLENDING ON THE LOOM

If you take two yarns together as weft and have three colours – say A, B and C – you can achieve gradation with the following method.

Start with two A yarns, weaving a few lines and replacing them with one strand A and one B, followed by two B, then one strand B and one C to two Cs. The effect will be a very soft change in shades rather than a jump, which can be effective when working with a number of colours.

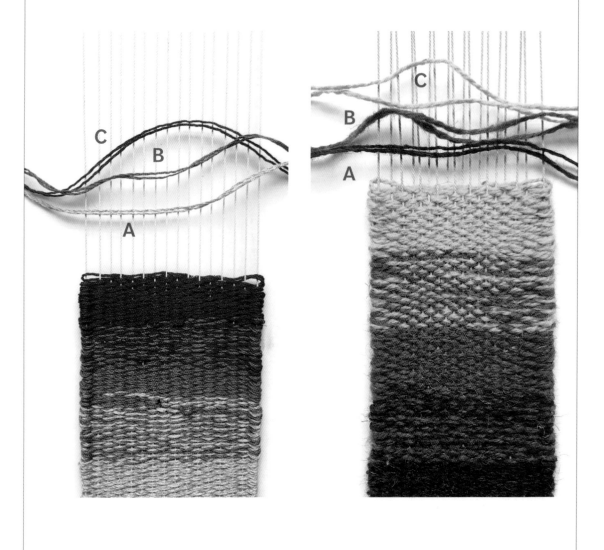

DOREEN GITTENS

Here I must mention my chance encounter with Doreen Gittens, an award-winning textile designer who specializes in handwoven textiles. She founded her company, Archipelago Textiles, 25 years ago. Based on London's South Bank, one of the original tenants of the iconic OXO Tower, it is there that Doreen weaves the most vibrant scarves and fabrics for interiors, using only the finest silk, wool and linen yarns. Her younger years were spent travelling and living on islands – Jamaica, Barbados, Grenada – before she settled back in the UK. Her fascination for textiles started early, under the influence of her dressmaker mother, and she eventually went on to pursue a Masters' degree in Design from Glasgow University.

My fortuitous meeting with Doreen led to a new friendship and creative inspiration, as well as the opportunity to step out of my home studio and share her studio for a year. That time in her studio was transformative – I realized how important it was for me to physically separate work and home life. Even after I had moved on to my own studio, Doreen's passion and dedication for her craft has been a continual inspiration. It's only fitting that this chapter on walking through the seasons shows her rich, timeless and colourful weaves.

61

Above: Hand-dyed silk, weaving in progress.
Right: Handwoven silk shawl, 100 × 200cm (39¼ × 78¾in).

Mimosa on a frame loom, cotton weft on a nylon monofilament warp with mimosa leaves.

MIMOSA

Mimosa is a celebration of the colour yellow with its equally beautiful blue-green leaves. The canary yellow pom-pom blooms are always such an overpowering delight in spring that I overlooked the leaves for a long time. Then, one perfect sunny morning, I was forced to pay attention when I observed the trimming of the tree on one of my walks near my studio; I was so stunned by its filigree-like foliage that the gardener, noticing my awe, stopped his work and offered me a few cuttings, which I lovingly pressed in the studio. And this weave was born.

HONESTY

Honesty is another seasonal delight for me. I love its seed pods, those moon-shaped, translucent papery discs always shimmering in the autumnal sun. I delight in splicing them open, releasing the seeds and seeing the inner disc with beautiful connecting marks that resemble delicate hand stitching.

September, 43 × 55cm (17 × 21¾in), framed. Handwoven with cotton, nettle yarn and honesty (*Lunaria annua*) seed pods.

NOTICER AND NOTICINGS

I capture the summer through my triptych
Noticer and Noticings. The riot of blue skies and
the long walks in the greens with bracken and
maple keys are incorporated into the weaves.

Noticer and Noticings triptych, 46 × 56cm (18¼ × 22in)
each. Handwoven with silk, cotton and linen yarns with
bracken, ruscus and maple keys.

Autumn Walk (detail).

AUTUMN WALK

Until I moved to London, I had never experienced the seasonal procession of golden, yellow, amber and scarlet leaves dropping off the trees and carpeting the cold, wet ground, with yellow leaves plastered on pavements like exquisite inlay work. The rust, gold and red-tinted leaves of autumn are a perfect enticement to lace up the boots and go out for a long, crisp walk. Walking on thick piles of London plane leaves always makes me smile no matter what else is going on. I am drawn to the earth colours that every fallen leaf gradually turns into, from various shades of dry, light brown to rich, wet, decaying deeper browns in the winter rains.

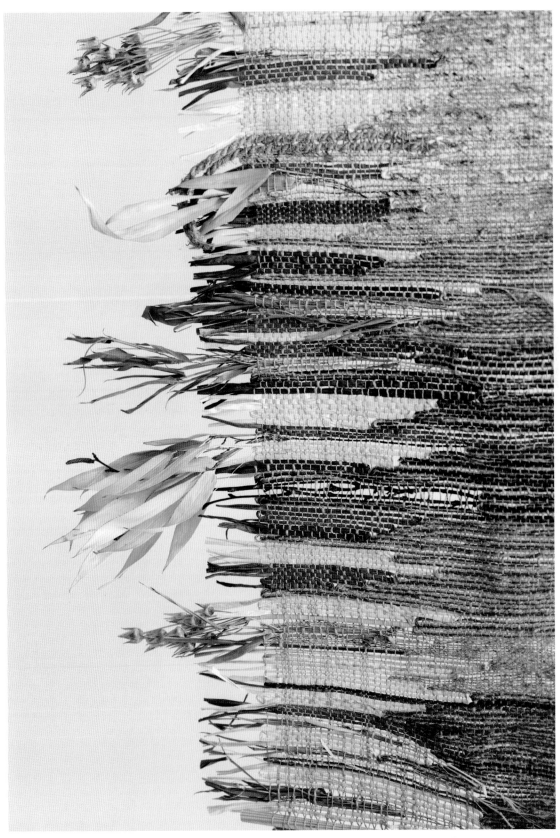

Opposite: *Summer's End*, 28 × 118cm (11 × 46½in). Woven on cottolin warp with various dried foliage. Detail shown above.

68

SHEILA AND I

Every yearly cycle I discover or rediscover the beauty of a particular tree, its leaves, flowers and fruits. What grabs me one year could be something simple, such as the opening of magnolia buds. If I let myself be immersed in the observation of the daily unfurling progress, even once in its life cycle, it is a bit like gaining a friend for life. I feel a deep emotional bond to that tree in particular, as well as to all magnolias in general.

No matter where you travel, to an unknown part of town or to a new country, if there is a familiar plant around you, you feel at home. This is the most fascinating element of nature. If you can find what is familiar, you never feel out of place; you never feel that you 'don't belong' or that you are in the wrong place at the wrong time.

Every moment spent in the company of trees and plants is refreshing and rewarding. I have spent hours, for example, admiring the camellia bush in my garden. There is a time every year when the little bush is full of flowers in all their phases: from a tight bud, to buds in various stages of opening, to the flower from young to very old and, finally, the most beautiful fallen flowers, with fading colours in countless shades of brown blanketing the earth all around the bush. This bush, in the brief period it encompasses the full life cycle through its flowers, is a perfect celebration of life.

'I have tried to delay the frosts, I have coaxed the fading flowers, I thought I could detain a few of the crimson leaves until you had smiled upon them; but their companions call them, and they cannot stay away.'

Emily Dickinson

Sheila and I (detail). A chance meeting with my favourite weaver Sheila Hicks in Paris inspired this weave. Handwoven with linen, wool, cotton yarns and various dried foliage.

Daily Commute (two shown here from a collection of six), 33.5 × 33.5cm (13 × 13in) each.
Photos taken on my daily commute to the studio, woven together.

(4)

DAILY COMMUTE

'Every day is a journey and the journey itself is home'

Matsuo Basho

Most of us commute or journey to a particular destination regularly, whether to work, school, a shop or a friend's or family member's home. For some, this recurrence can generate a form of boredom, while for others, it offers a quiet pleasure and a familiar consolation. On my more frequent sojourns I turn the walk into a complete visual activity, thinking over the sights and assimilating the new into the accustomed.

When walking a familiar terrain, where no navigation is required, it is natural for the body and mind to fall into a rhythm of thinking in motion. Each walk weaves into a continuous textured experience. I love to scrutinize a particular pathway, for example, and tune into the direction of the wind, any change of light, cast shadows, the world around me reflected in puddles (frequent in the UK!). I see new graffiti on the wall where the pigeon sits cooing, the bird's iridescent neck shimmering in the sun, its feathers ruffling in the breeze. Deep yellow lichens crop up on stone walls, bark and twigs. Cumulus clouds chase each other, and pampas grass swings with its delicate white flowers.

Daily Commute: Photographs of a pigeon and algae are woven together.

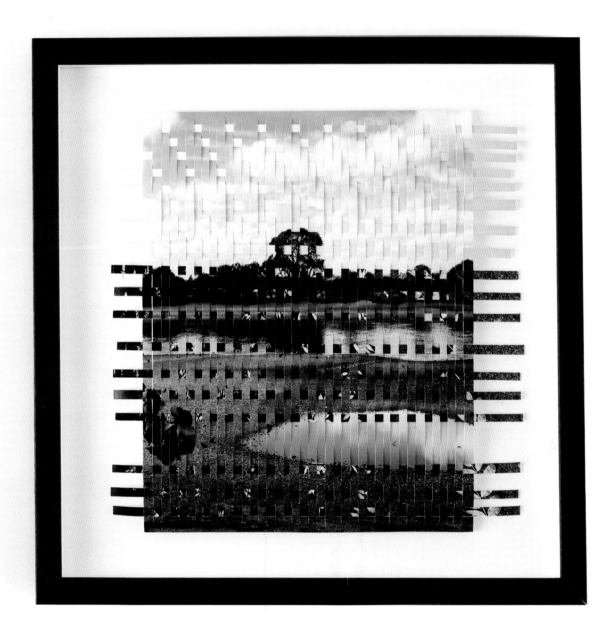

Daily Commute: Photographs of low tide
on the River Thames and wind-blown
leaves are woven together.

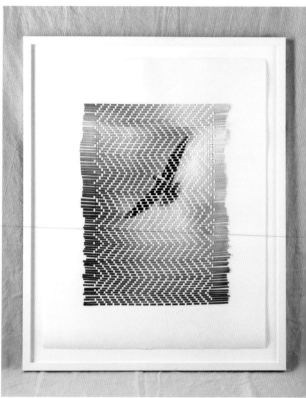

EVERYDAY OBSERVATIONS

These observations are often forgotten in the chaos of everyday life, but recording these ordinary sights through photographs allows me to reflect later on my observations from a particular walk, and to reminisce over the passage of time – a week, a month, a year, or more – how everything or nothing is the same depending on my mood. Being outside, paying attention to familiar surroundings, lets me look at ordinary objects with fresh eyes and appreciate their beauty and wonder, which is what I need to be creative within my studio walls. These photos, once printed, become inspiration and material to capture a story and freeze it in time.

For a whole year, I was lucky to have a studio by the river. My daily commute became quite exciting. I started to record my everyday observations. Looking back at those photos, I was interested to start seeing what was impossible to capture in one photo – the barking dog behind me, for instance, or the same view, which had such different hues from one day to the next. There was the flutter of wings the moment I tried to capture birds on camera, the gulls circling overhead as I busily recorded the still, reflecting river, disturbed only by swans and a few yellow leaves bobbing in the water.

Opposite, left: *Swan*, 93 × 115cm (36½ × 45¼in). Paper as warp and photo as weft woven in a diamond twill pattern.
Opposite, right: *Gull*, 93 × 115cm (36½ × 45¼in). Paper as warp and photo as weft woven in a twill pattern.
Left: *Goose*, 93 × 115cm (36½ × 45¼in). Paper as warp and photo as weft woven in a twill pattern.
Below: Experiments in weaving with various printed papers, photos and painted canvas.

PHOTO WEAVING

Towards the end of my art residency, I thought of working with all the photos I had taken during my commute to the studio each day. The idea of weaving these photos together physically almost felt like connecting and giving meaning to all those hours I had spent walking that path, thinking those thoughts.

Selecting the photos and the type of weaving pattern is a crucial part of the design process. A single photo can be approached in various ways. I will share my methods of weaving the photos here.

WEAVING PHOTOS WITH PLAIN PAPER

This is a method where vertically cut strips of plain thick paper act as the warp and horizontal strips of photos become the weft. I personally prefer not to cut the paper all the way, leaving a few centimetres at least at one end, but I also love the uneven extra layer of texture that can be created by working with unattached strips. I number the strips of weft to make following the pattern easier and to avoid the image becoming jumbled. One can use a combination of weaving techniques to either show the paper more or the photo more, depending on what is desired. A lot of interesting geometrical patterns can be created while weaving this, especially if one is using a solid-coloured paper.

 **+**  **=**

ONE SUBJECT

I take a landscape and a portrait format of the same view, to depict the blurry quality between the quotidian and the gradual passing of time. The portrait format is cut into vertical strips to act as the warp and the landscape format becomes the weft by cutting into horizontal strips. Here the possibilities are immense. Imagination is key. One can experiment with the widths of the cut strips and the types of weaving patterns.

77

COMBINING VIEWS

I like to combine two very different views to depict the constantly changing surroundings of a commute where sights merge into each other. I use a combination of images, which I find a very pleasurable way of navigating the terrain of daily life. It keeps my mind aware of my immediate surroundings and inspires me with new ideas and possibilities.

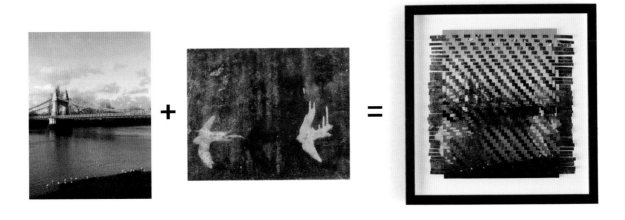

Are We There Yet?, 50 × 76cm (19¾ × 30in), woven using the cover page from the book
On the Other Side of the Forest, which holds special and nostalgic significance for the artist.

I-CHUN JENKINS

I had the privilege of coming across the splendid paper weaves by Canadian fibre artist I-Chun Jenkins. Using recycled books and magazines, she meticulously cuts, splices, weaves, crochets and folds the pages to create unique, colourful structures. From her studio in Rusagonis, New Brunswick, she draws on the beauty and inspiration of nature and jazz music. Oscillating between memories of her childhood in Taiwan and her current life in Canada, she merges these two unique cultures in her life and her work to create intricate, imaginative surfaces charged with mystery and distinct narrative.

State of Mind, 50cm × 76cm (19¾ × 30in). Woven using old books and magazines, depicting the constant frenzy of looking for new ideas and inspiration.

Are We There Yet? (detail).

Just as no one learns to ride a bike from a manual, it is difficult to learn to weave from a book. To really develop and refine your craft, you need to hone your creative skills; to do this, quite simply, it is important to create every day. The more you experiment with types of images, size of cut strips, and weaves, the better chance you have of turning the final pieces into your own original works of art.

WOVEN CANVASES

While collecting 'waste materials' from art studios to design a workshop on weaving with these materials, I was given a couple of old painted canvases by artist Vanessa Raw. For three years, I could not bear to cut them, but eventually I did, metamorphosing them into another form. The power of weaving is immense and experiments like this are especially fun.

Cutting up these painted faces, each weft having the power to alternate the original image, is almost akin to the fragility of us humans altered by thoughts beyond our control, like traversing a beautiful internal landscape. Repeating the most basic pattern in weaving (one up, one down) is a calming and meditative act, quite natural and freeing.

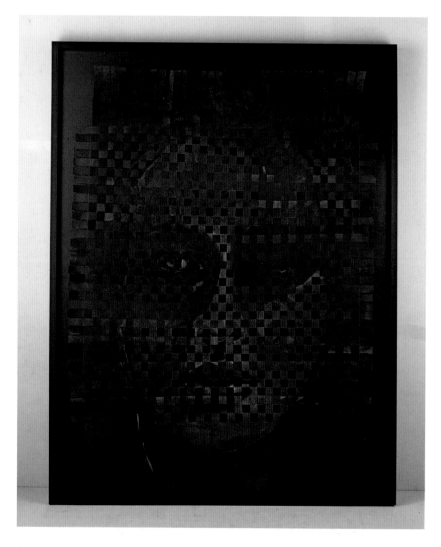

Untitled 1, 120 × 155cm (47¼ × 61in). Handwoven from strips of oil-painted canvas.

Untitled 2, 105cm × 130cm (41¼ × 51in). Woven from strips of oil-painted canvas.

MEDITATIVE WALKING

Encounters of repetition are usually bound with a sense of enchantment. While delighting in the presence of discernible patterns, textures, sounds, colours and smells, I am also charmed by surprises that break the order. They disrupt the familiar so as to inject wonder, awe and curiosity into our daily commute, like a sudden foggy morning blanketing the whole landscape, or a splendid sunset bathed in hues from heather to crimson to gold.

It is quite strange how walking can so quickly wander into philosophy, spirituality, cultures and family sagas. We have an innate capacity for remembering and imagining places, and when walking a familiar path, perception, memory, imagination and the present path are in constant interaction. I get carried away sometimes, losing my sense of time and space and getting entangled in two places at once. This journey of foot and mind creates interesting visuals inside my head. They are quick to come and go and are easily missed if I do not make a note of them.

My personal thoughts often dwell on the duality of my life: my childhood and early adulthood in India and my current life in London. The colours of a blossom, graffiti, a leaf blowing in the wind, any random image or motion can make my reflections cross hundreds of miles, transporting me to all the places I have called home. Looking deep into the centre of a daisy, for instance, makes me think of rich yellow marigolds, carrying me back to the flower markets in India. The present fuses with memory and, at times, fantasy.

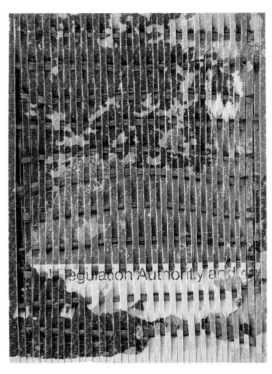

Top left, top middle and top right: *Duality: I See Flowers Everywhere.*
Puddle + lotus; daisy + marigold; embroidery + magnolia.
Above left: *Graffiti 1/London.*
Above right: *Graffiti 2/India.*

Adrift. Handwoven photographs of swifts and clouds in a summer sky.

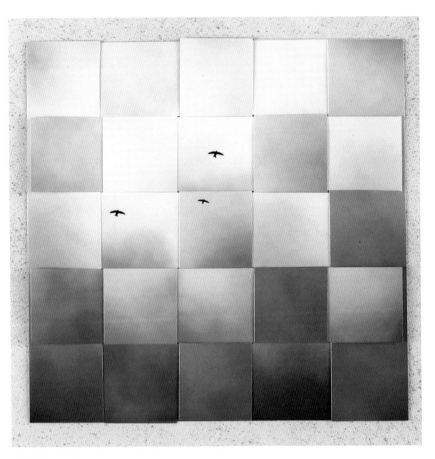

Adrift (detail).

Over time, I find walking an almost meditative ritual, an investigation of the deeply personal terrains inside the mind. It is a freeing activity, letting me ponder even the heaviest thoughts with buoyancy and lightness. My mind quietly wanders from new plans to recollections to observation, swaying between the present and the past while being in touch with the future. The shortest of walks can help me arrive at surprising revelations and clarifications.

Walking is also freeing because it allows me to think without being busy with my thoughts. I am lucky to have a brush with botany every time I step out onto the pavement. This is where my love affair with the flora of London began; the natural fragments that peep out at us from the cracks and crevices, waiting to be discovered and admired. It is most joyful paying attention to these tiny growths, even on busy days. I am notified of changes in the nature diary by leaves, flowers, sepals and seed pods that carpet the pavements carried by the breeze from gardens, parks and houses nearby.

86

Journal with photos and ideas for *Pavement Botanics* and a woven sample with nettle, hemp, cotton and jute yarns on a nettle warp.

The most uneven pavements sometimes end up protecting the most delicate feathers or the brightest eucalyptus leaves from being trodden on and successfully making their way into my studio. I love the surprise of finding vivid flowers swaying in the morning breeze from the tiniest cracks on walls: they offer a daily lesson in resilience.

These observations led to the weaving of the pieces I call 'pavement botanics'. They are a stylized depiction of the cracks and growth I encounter daily out on the streets. These little crevices filled with such brightness and promise of life inspire me every day.

For me, the repetitive act of weaving allows a freedom to muse on subjects related or unrelated to what is being woven. In those transcendent moments, sitting at the loom, I experience an intense happiness and freedom, intuiting that this is the work I am meant to be doing and the life I am meant to be leading. Becoming absorbed in the mundanity of this commute supported the act of creation. Surrounded by my woven pieces and looking at my notebook brimming with new ideas, I realize how joyful and essential the journey to this place has been to my creative process.

Pavement Botanics. Woven with raffia, nettle and cotton yarn on a nettle warp.

'There is more to life than simply increasing its speed.'

Mahatma Gandhi

Memory Containers. Woven baskets using grass, flax, sisal, cotton, paper and jute.

(5)

A WALK DOWN
MEMORY LANE

'Remembrance of things past is not necessarily
the remembrance of things as they were.'

Marcel Proust

It has been said that memories are not fixed or frozen but are transformed, assembled and reassembled with every act of recollection. Human memory is imperfect. It arises not only from direct experience but from many other factors: what we read, what we were told, what others say or think. Every recollection alters or transforms memory, giving space for creativity, imagination and storytelling, which I love. I have had raging 'wars' with my siblings on various occasions when each of us recall our own 'true' version of the same incident from our childhood.

For me, memories and possessions are closely related. I often wonder what compels us to keep things we do not need in cupboards, drawers, shelves and attics. Sometimes they are neatly filed, keepsakes in between pages of books, precious, special items – a photograph, a ticket stub, stamps, envelopes, and old letters, pressed flowers in a book, faded notes from long ago, children's drawings, fragments of old textiles, a shell, a rock, twigs – all of these personal items have an immense power to evoke memories and emotional connections.

Objects we cherish surpass their initial function. They are imbued with a new meaning and provide a sense of security and safety. Uncertainties in our lives make us more nostalgic about the past. And, for me, having called multiple places 'home' has made me hoard such 'trigger' objects; in my house and my studio, my 18-year-old self lives side by side with my current self. I love it when I open a book and a chocolate wrapper, a pressed flower or a handwritten grocery list from long ago falls from between the pages.

These are perfect moments to reminisce about days long gone and I relish every minute. Perhaps we retain these objects as we can't retain time. These items jog our memory and link us to places, moments and people – a witness to and reminder of the past.

90

Right: *Nostalgia* (detail). Handwoven with mainly cotton and wool yarn on a nylon monofilament warp, incorporating old ticket stubs, fragments from envelopes and other mementos.
Opposite: *Nostalgia*. Work in progress on a handbuilt pipe loom.

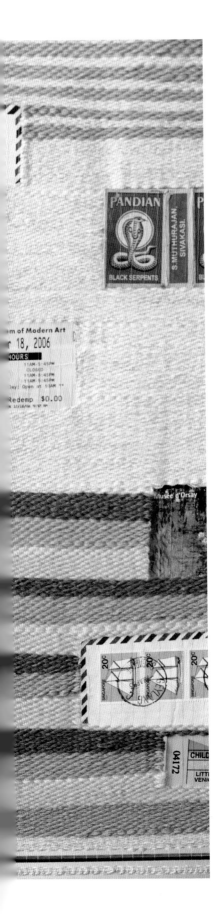

INSPIRATION
FROM MEMORY

It's said that we leave something of ourselves behind when we leave a place, and there are things in us that we can find again by going back there. In this chapter, I will explore woven works that remind me of a person, an era, a place or a feeling. Drawing from natural, man-made, found, cherished and repurposed elements, I explore those nameless feelings that take a more concrete form in these woven pieces. I swing between a deep longing to recreate lost moments and simply taking pleasure in the present experience of a memory without fretting that we cannot relive those moments.

FAYE'S FLOWERS

Most of us have experienced the curious phenomenon of obsessing over a thing or thought then starting to see that 'thing' everywhere: in conversations, in people's homes, shops, books, magazines. *Faye's Flowers* was woven straight after one of my trips to India, where I had visited the spice plantations in the south. I was fascinated by pepper vines growing on the farms there. These delicate creepers, entwined around trees for support, with their glossy green leaves, laden with yellow-red fruits, were very picturesque.

Coincidentally, on my return, I chanced upon a London florist called Faye who had peppercorns in her little shop. I was compelled to make these weaves with those dried red and white peppercorns that reminded me so much of India. The peppercorns were far from home (like me), and their purpose had altered from a spice to an ornament or decoration.

Opposite, above: *Faye's Flowers 1 and 2*, 42 × 52cm (16½ × 20½in), framed. Handwoven using wool, silk, cotton and linen yarns with red and white dried peppercorns.
Opposite, left and right: *Faye's Flowers 1 and 2* (detail).

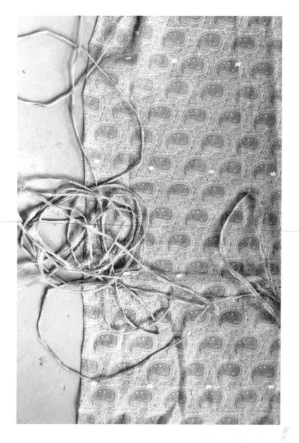

MAAJI KI SARI

Maaji ki sari ('Grandma's sari') was woven from strips of my grandmother's sari, combined with other yarns, weaving and meditating on a precious life, lived with grace, warmth and love. Memory is a static term, whereas 'remembering' is a dynamic process that leads to creative storytelling. Remembering transforms memories; they are disassembled and reassembled with each recollection.

While preparing the sari yarn, touching and holding my grandmother's sari, ripping it and weaving with it, I have consciously remembered my grandmother. My recollected moments have gone through many versions and I feel that my memories of her have strengthened and become more powerful. I realized that I could actually recall a multitude of memories I didn't even know I possessed. It makes me happy to have thought of her so much and so intently that I almost feel her presence even a decade after she left us.

94

Above left: Grandma's old sari is ripped into thin strips to form lengths of yarn.
Left: Weaving in progress with the sari yarn along with linen and cotton yarn on a cotton warp.

Maaji ki Sari, 50 × 50cm (19¾ × 19¾). Handwoven on a cotton warp with a combination of linen, cotton, jute and sari yarn.

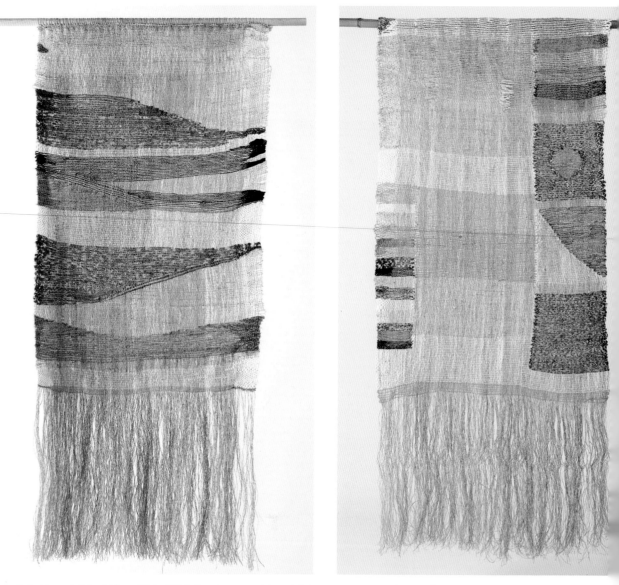

Above left: *Home 1*, 66 × 140cm (26 × 55in). Handwoven with mainly hemp, cotton and waste fabric yarn on a hemp warp. Above right: *Home 2*, 70 × 150cm (27½ × 59in). Handwoven with mainly hemp, cotton, jute, raffia and yarn from waste fabric on a hemp warp.

HOME

Home 1 and *Home 2* are woven pieces without the reed, to give fluidity to the hemp warp. I wove these pieces from my London studio while absorbed in thoughts of my parents, siblings and friends in India. The indigo is an old bed sheet my mother had gifted me more than a decade ago that has been cut into strips; the white and the red is from an old sari that had witnessed some very happy times. The geometry used in *Home 2* is loosely based on the floor plan of my new home in London, which the rest of my family in India are yet to visit.

MAKING YARNS OUT OF OLD SHEETS OR WASTE FABRIC

• Make notches along the selvedge for the desired width of the fabric strip.

• Tear along until the end. You can use scissors, but I like the frayed edges you get with tearing.

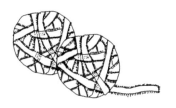

• Once you have all your strips ready, clean off the few hanging pieces of thread from the tearing. You can either start to weave with them, attaching them on the loom by overlapping both ends in the shed as you weave along, or join them by stitching with hand or machine, either straight or diagonal, as shown below, to prepare continuous weft for larger weaves.

Stitch along the dotted lines.

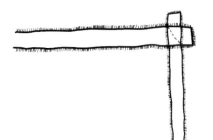

Stitch along the dotted lines. Trim off extra fabric.

BAZAAR

Every visit to India is full of so much colour, love, warmth, food and shopping that my piece *Bazaar* essentially wove itself on my return from one such trip. In this piece I have tried to capture the vibrancy of the fruit and vegetable markets: the chaos and confusion of crowds, the haggling and noise of everyone talking over each other, the abundance of colourful fruits and vegetables in all their shades – overall, it is a very happy place.

Above left: *Bazaar*, detail of tassels made from high-twist fabric ropes. Above right: *Bazaar*, detail of yellow cotton warp and plain weave incorporating recycled fabric ropes in bright colours.

Bazaar, 80 × 110cm (31½ × 43¼). Handwoven in bright cotton yarns incorporating wood and ropes made from recycled fabric.

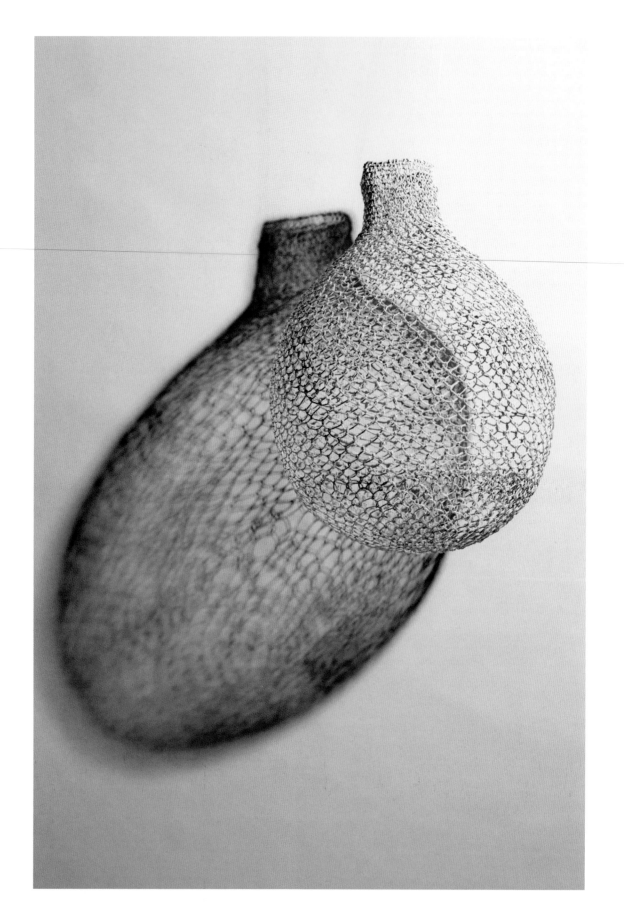

CLOISTERED

A weaver's world is closely connected to the world of other fibre techniques, such as knitting, crochet, looping and netting; as a maker, I am frequently drawn to these other techniques. *Cloistered* is an investigation of those private, innermost feelings of nostalgia and ache that are hard to describe in words. I have used circular knitting with paper yarns in various earth colours. The open structure and lightness of form creates an interesting play of shadows with the slightest movement, an invitation for wistful thoughts to come and go.

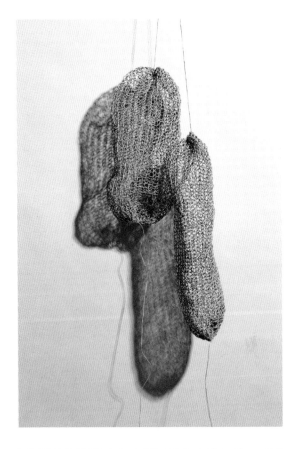

Opposite: *Void*. Looping technique with paper yarn, created using a balloon.
Right: *Cloistered*. Circular knitting with paper yarn.

Mela, 55 × 55cm (21¾ × 21¾in). Hand-stitched strips of bright silk fabric woven together.

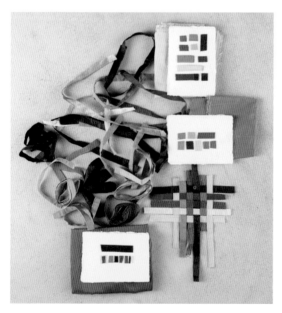

Work in progress, playing with colours and ideas.

MELA

Mela is a collaboration with Vineyard Community in Richmond, a charity that helps people overcome personal crises and reconnect with society. It runs a sewing project called Works of Love, which offers a welcoming environment for women in challenging situations to come together and learn new skills. With the help of manager Cornelia Costeanu and volunteer Ermelinda Da Costa, we prepared strips of silk fabrics to weave a vibrant piece. It echoes the bustle of Patna (the town in northern India where I was born), where rickshaws, scooters, bicycles and cars go speeding along, creating an atmosphere akin to a carnival or a funfair, 'Mela' in Hindi.

ERROLL PIRES NELSON

Ply-split braiding is a lesser-known textile technique where one cord passes through another cord, splitting the plies. It's not to be confused with crochet, macramé or knitting. Ply-split braiding is used to construct camel girths and animal regalia in western India. Intricate geometric patterning and figured motifs are found in the girths ('tang' in the local language). The girth is used to secure the saddle on the camel. The materials used are goat hair, camel hair and sometimes cotton cord. The technique is on the decline and efforts are being made to keep the languishing craft alive.

Erroll Pires Nelson, my teacher at the National Institute of Design (NID) in India, introduced me to the world of ply-split braiding. Going into Erroll's cabin/office was like entering an enchanted forest with bright, colourful, intricate and innovatively braided hangings on the walls. His passion of more than 35 years for this technique has created one-of-a-kind seamless dresses, bags and containers, and has given a contemporary application to the technique. Erroll has now retired from NID but conducts workshops around the world. He is a member of the Braid Society in the UK and participates and conducts workshops at international braiding conferences. I have included his details in the resources if you would like to learn more about him.

Shown below are a couple of Erroll's pieces and an illustration to explain the basic principle of ply-split braiding.

Splittee

Splitter

Far left: 10 x 20cm (4 x 8in), 4-ply cotton, plain oblique twining (POT) with perforations. Left: 10 x 152.5cm (4 x 60in), 2-ply dyed cotton cord, plain oblique twining (POT) with variations.

MEMORY CONTAINERS

Textile earth vessels, or 'memory containers', as I like to call them, use diverse techniques of weaving, twining, looping and netting. I feel that these fascinating techniques can be explored further, especially when one is creating yarns out of waste paper, plastics and fabrics, giving room to be more creative with further ideas and expressions.

My memory containers are a safe place for me to park my memories, old and new, and access them by holding and touching them. They recall the time I was making them and also bring to life the thoughts I had during the process of creation.

I am constantly exploring the mental landscape we create through the imaginative reconstruction of the universe that surrounds us, the places and people that confront us and all the objects that meet our gaze and occupy our minds. I often muse on how we experience time through materials; how we store memories in our mind and inject life into inanimate objects. Memory arises not only from our direct experiences but from the interaction of many minds – what we are told, what we read, what others say. This constant transformation, with each recollection giving room for creativity, is one I return to time and again in my studio.

'Memory is the diary that we all carry about with us.'

Oscar Wilde

Memory Containers (detail).

Memory Containers. Handwoven using grass, flax, sisal, cotton, paper and jute with birch twigs and other dried foliage.

Ode to Sylvia Plath. Weave inspired by a passage from Sylvia Plath's novel *The Bell Jar*.

(6)

WALK WITH A POEM IN YOUR HEART

'But words are things, and a small drop of ink, falling like dew, upon a thought,
Produces that which makes thousands, perhaps millions, think.'

Lord Byron

Literature has an ability to spark imagination, allowing the reader to interpret a book's mood, characters and the world they inhabit. Carefully chosen words paint visuals for the mind. This inspires other mediums of artistic expression. Since antiquity, literature in all its genres has inspired artists to retell a story with lines, colours and threads. There has always been cross-pollination between visual art and literature. Reading about nature helps express how the mind views nature and, at times, how the mind sees itself. It helps to understand how we use nature to understand ourselves; it definitely helps me.

We are all influenced by an immeasurable collection of thoughts and ideas – from writers, thinkers, poets and singers – and gain wisdom and the responsibility to live thoughtfully and intelligently. Their words teach us to enjoy, to question, to observe and to be patient with ourselves as well as the rest of the world.

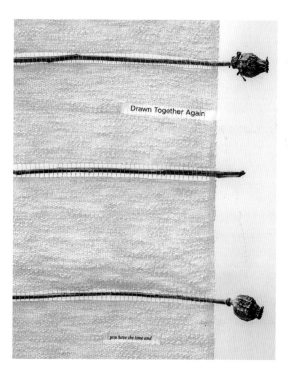

Above left and right: *Pods and Cocoons* (details).

Pods and Cocoons, 55 × 130cm (21¾ × 51in). Handwoven with cotton linen slub yarn incorporating dried poppy pods and printed paper with words.

INSPIRATION
FROM LITERATURE

Some writers bring such a poet's eye for detail to their descriptions that all my senses get activated and I sit straighter, breathe deeper and am almost compelled to write down that phrase or sentence in my notebook so I can go back to it again and again. Sometimes ideas for a new body of work germinate while reading. Often the titles of a completed work stare at me from a random book; it was always there, in black and white, tucked by my bedside. I have several journals where I copy down phrases that move me.

Written words make me think. They change my behaviour; I pay closer attention to the elements around me, the wind, the sounds, the leaves, the earth I step on. They lay bare the grounds of my emotional attachment to the natural world. A good poem encourages an intimate scrutiny of self and recognizes feelings that help in naming and firming half-formed ideas. This joyful celebration of my external and internal landscape, in turn, creates a kind of magical enchantment in my studio that spurs my creative expressions. While weaving, I listen to podcasts or audio books; I feel that the regular rhythm of the spoken word makes my weaving go faster.

110

Left: *Safety Jacket* (detail). Paper poetry yarn is wrapped around sisal to create the knotted safety clasp. Opposite, above: *Safety Jacket*, 45 × 110cm (17¾ × 43¼in). Hand-stitched barkcloth with poetry yarn clasp, inspired by the poetry of Mary Oliver.

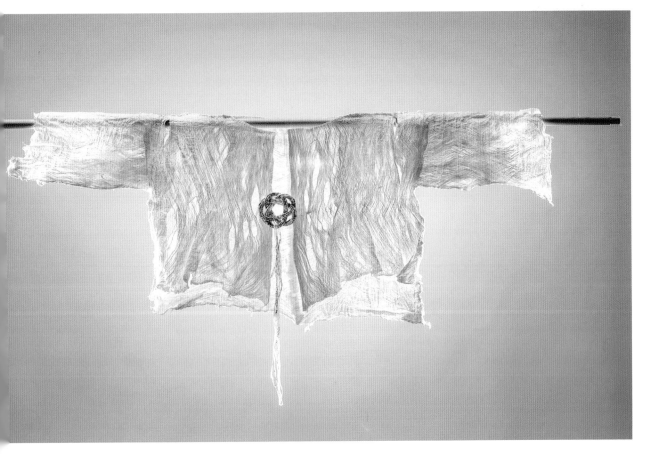

I take these influences and teachings on my walks, meditating on them. I learn to dream, imagine, wander and wonder with them, embracing uncertainties and doubts – it's a significant part of my creative practice. Mary Oliver's wise words, for instance, have been a tonic for my heart and never fail to strike my mind into action with zest and energy. Her poetry articulates difficult-to-express emotions in a simple, humble manner while encouraging a slowness that very much appeals to the weaver in me.

Safety Jacket is a piece of work directly influenced by Oliver's words. Inspired by her love for and close attention to the natural world, I hand stitched this safety jacket out of mulberry bark. Her book *A Thousand Mornings* is one of my favourites. I wrote down her poems on large mulberry paper and later cut the paper lengthwise into 5mm (¼in) strips, leaving them attached at both ends. Then I put them between dampened towels, rolled them on textured stones and spun them on my drop spindle to prepare a precious spool of poetry yarn. Wrapping sisal cord in poetry yarn, I then knotted the sisal to create a clasp for the safety jacket, which acts like a talisman, protecting the wearer from the harshness of the world. It's a reminder of the abundance of natural beauty that surrounds us and of our duty to love and protect it.

SUSAN BYRD

While attempting to hand spin and create my own paper yarns with handwritten poetry for weaving, I started studying about *shifu*, a Japanese textile woven from thread made with paper. I chanced upon Susan Byrd's book, *A Song of Praise for Shifu*, which gives a thorough look at the history, technique and design of shifu.

Several decades have passed since Susan was awarded an apprenticeship fellowship to study shifu with Sadako Sakurai, an internationally renowned shifu weaver. Many of the makers Susan encountered while in Japan are now deceased or are no longer working in the craft, but a few continue to make their own paper threads and weave, including her teacher Sadako Sakurai, now in her nineties.

According to Susan, this ancient craft has touched the lives of many people through the centuries, in Japan as well as those in other countries who have been captivated by its intrinsic beauty. She explains that shifu's allure is rooted in the various techniques used to make a thread from paper and, of course, in the finished cloth itself, whether made for

112

Dampened paper from a Nō plays script book, ready to be rolled. A single sheet of paper, measuring approx. 22 × 32.5cm (8¾ × 12¾in) was cut into strips 2cm (approx. ¾in) wide.

Rolled and separated paper threads in a basket, and the spun threads lying wrapped around bamboo spools on a straw mat. The spinning wheel is a Japanese itoguruma.

clothing to wear or as an art piece. Originally, Susan says, there were two distinctive types of shifu: everyday work clothes for the working class, often made from recycled account book or textbook pages; and a more refined cloth that was made into summer kimonos and other attire for the elite. Susan hopes that the skills of the few dedicated craftspeople left today will continue to be passed on to help preserve this time-honoured textile for future generations.

Here are a few images from Susan showing the preparing and weaving with the paper yarns from account books from Japan as weft and a warp of cotton, creating *menjifu* ('men' is short for 'momen', which means 'cotton', while 'jifu' means 'paper cloth').

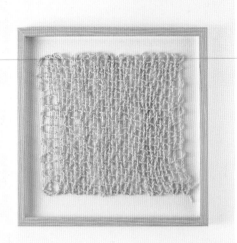

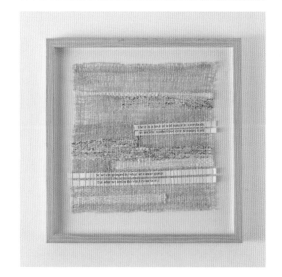

THE ORDINARY MIND: FEELING, BELONGING, BEING

The Ordinary Mind: Feeling, Belonging, Being is a set of nine weaves (only five shown here) using poetry yarns, printed paper, newspaper and grass, which represents the enormity and also the simplicity of the world we live in. While hand spinning paper and making cords, I also started exploring cordages from grass, nettle, rhubarb, blackcurrant stems, iris and daffodil leaves, which opened even more possibilities for adding textures to the simplest weaves.

I derive much joy in the process, from gathering the raw materials to making the cordages; the world slows down and I become immersed in the repetitive, rhythmic twisting as I form the cordage. In the resources, I have listed a few courses and online tutorials for some basic information on working with these materials.

The technique of making cordages is the same as for the plastic cordages explained in the River Walk chapter, explained on page 43. I love the fact that this technique does not require many tools and is so simple to grasp that one can happily spend hours creating a few metres of cordage.

Left and opposite: *The Ordinary Mind: Feeling, Belonging, Being*, each piece 25 × 25cm (9¾ × 9¾in). Left, top to bottom: Handspun newspaper, handspun grass, paper poetry yarn with strips of printed poetry, handwoven paper poetry yarn. Opposite: Woven map with cotton linen slub yarn.

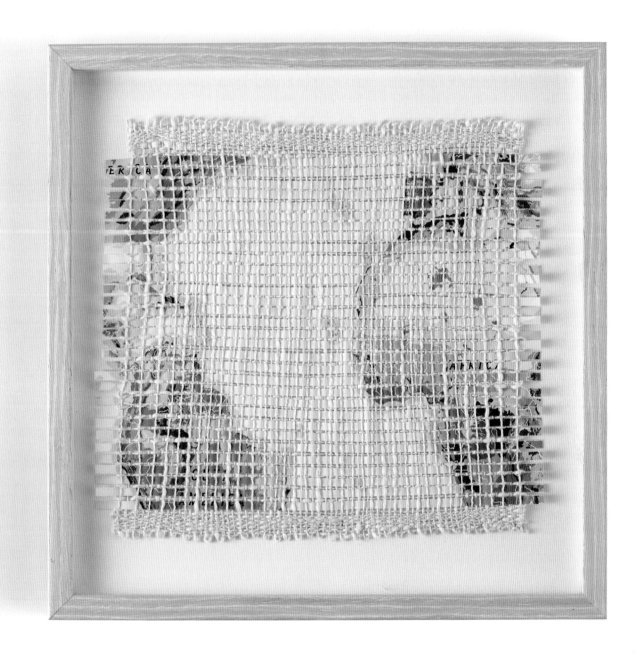

ODE TO SYLVIA PLATH

One day in the studio, my artist friend Monica gave me a fig leaf from her garden. The leaf reminded me of a passage from Sylvia Plath's *The Bell Jar*, where a fig tree becomes a symbol of the life choices that the protagonist faces. She imagines that each fig represents a different life; she can only choose one fig but, paralyzed with indecision, the figs rot and fall to the ground.

The fig tree represents an inner turmoil between conforming to the expected role of a young woman and the desire to be an individual. Women are confronted by such a bewildering variety of seeming possibilities that choice itself becomes all but impossible. This continues to be a common dilemma for women today.

Ode to Sylvia Plath is a piece inspired by the beauty of this passage and the poignancy of the tragic end in store for the writer. Dried fig leaf has been woven in the piece with a mix of wool, cotton and linen yarns all around it.

Ode to Sylvia Plath. Cotton warp and a mix of cotton, linen and wool as weft, incorporating a fig leaf into the weave. Displayed on the frame loom.

Fragments, 60 × 90cm (23½ × 35½in). Handwoven paper souvenir bags pieced together on Kozo paper.

FRAGMENTS

I also love the beautifully produced book *The Gorgeous Nothings*, which is the first full-colour facsimile of Emily Dickinson's manuscripts exactly as she wrote them, on scraps of envelopes. It offers a glimpse into the process of one of the world's most creative minds.

Fragments is a combination of collage and weaving using paper bags collected from my travels. It reminds me of the places I've been to and the great art I've seen, which have inspired my own creations.

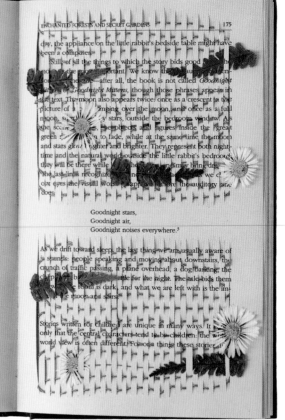

In Praise of Books, the book page as warp with linen yarn, daisy and bracken as weft.

IN PRAISE OF BOOKS

We humans have a deep need to understand who we are; we want to communicate, connect and preserve moments and events, real or imagined. We read or write to overcome our loneliness and to feel one with the width and depth of this enormous globe. Our longing for mutuality is met when we read and are touched by a thought that might have been written centuries ago. It unites all living beings and widens our boundaries. Words inspire me and help keep me balanced. They motivate, awaken and encourage the feelings and emotions that I need to be creative.

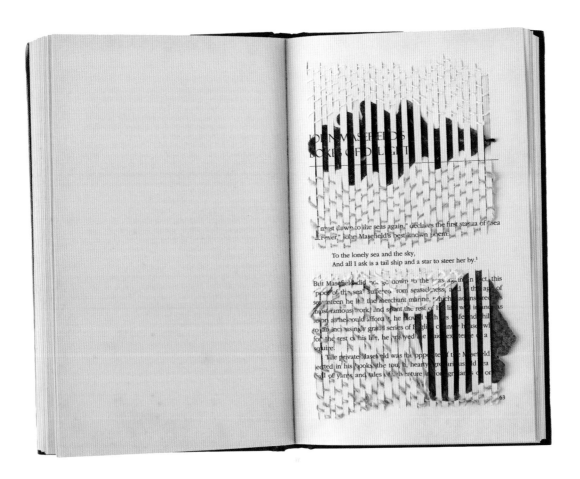

In Praise of Books, the book page as warp with cotton, linen, oak and gingko leaf as weft.

CONCLUSION

Creativity has many ways of taking shape. Making with my own two hands gives intangible ideas a certain form and a beginning. It is this giving birth to a new concept that is, perhaps, the most joyous part of the act for me.

Looking back through my journey through this book – by woodland and rivers, through seasons and memory, to my studio and with poetry in my heart – I have realized that, for me, materials are vital. New ideas emerge from the natural and, indeed, man-made materials I see on my walks – gathered, foraged, scavenged, salvaged, carefully sourced, hoarded, collected or photographed. From a papery seed pod to an old, yellowed, translucent paper bag to a sky full of swifts or the captivating flow of the river, not only do I use these materials for inspiration, I literally weave them into my pieces, creating art while exploring new ways of displaying and sharing them.

I hope that by reading this book, you have not only come to appreciate weaving in a new way, but have found inspiration to plunge into your own discoveries. To go out and explore old, new and historic techniques – to develop and further your own creative journey.

'When we lie down in the meadow, an ear pressed to the earth, or lean out from the bridge over the water, or gaze long and long into the brilliant sky, this is our way of listening to it, the huge serene heart, and it is the heart of the mother, whose children we are.'

Hermann Hesse

Dried foliage ready for weaving.

WEAVING BASICS

Weaving is one of the most ancient crafts. It emerged to serve a basic need of mankind – protection from the elements – by providing clothing and shelter. Over time, the craft has been mechanized and digitized through machines and computers, but the basic principles of weaving remain unchanged.

Weaving is simply the interlacing of two elements: the vertical threads in tension, called warp, and the horizontal, moveable threads, called weft. A plain weave is the passing of weft between alternately raised warps.

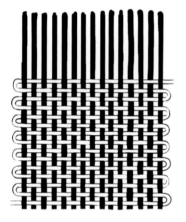

Plain weave: The weft thread is passed over a warp thread and under the next warp thread consecutively.

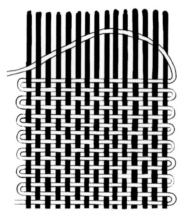

In order to not over-tighten the weft thread and create a regular selvedge (the left and right edges of the weaving), it is important to arch the weft yarn instead of pulling it straight (also known as 'bubbling' or 'rainbow').

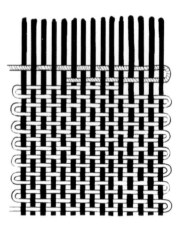

To add a new weft yarn in the case of changing colour, or when the weft yarn in the bobbin is finished, lay the new yarn in the open shed with a little overlap to the old weft yarn. The loose ends are taken to the back of the weave.

USING TOOLS

The most basic requirements for weaving are:
• Tension on warp
• Raising of warp (alternate, or a particular order depending on the design)
• Passing of weft

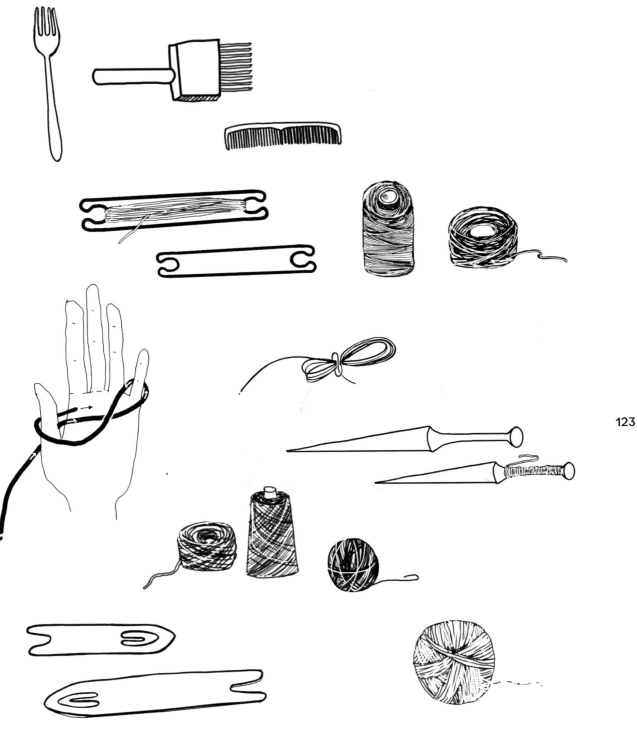

From top to bottom: Common fork, tapestry fork and plastic comb for beating weft yarn; flat shuttles, butterfly shuttle (made by wrapping weft yarn in a figure of eight around the fingers), tapestry bobbins and netting shuttles. Weft is wound onto shuttles for ease in weaving. The shape and size of shuttles and bobbins determine its usage together with personal preference. I love to use a butterfly shuttle for smaller weaves and techniques such as soumak.

Tension on warp

A loom is a device that helps create tension in the warp yarns for ease in weaving. Looms can be as simple as a piece of cardboard with notches or a wooden frame, to more complex backstrap looms or bigger floor looms with beams to wrap whole yardages of warp yarn.

Raising of warp

The raising of warp threads or creating a shed (for weft yarn to pass) is achieved with the help of heddles (string or metal); the design of these differ based on the type of loom. A simple shedding mechanism can be attached to a basic wooden or metal frame loom for efficient weaving.

Passing of weft

The passing of weft through the warp can be achieved using various tools – for example, bobbins, shuttles and butterflies – to which weft yarn of considerable length can be wound and carried from one end of the warp width to the other without becoming tangled.

THE JOY OF WEAVING

I was taught to weave cloth at design school in India more than 20 years ago. We were trained to develop innovative and original woven designs that could be mass-produced by design houses around the world. I was always drawn to the 'making by hand' part and the simplicity of the basic principles of weaving. My personal practice has evolved to a more 'art-led' approach. Over the years I've been learning how to express my daily experiences through the medium of weaving, using minimal tools and doing very simple weaves.

Exploring weaving is such a rewarding, fun and fulfilling activity for me. I love experimenting and discovering how the same weaves can have very different appearances depending on the thickness of the warp and the weft, the number of warps per inch (how dense or open the warp is) and the beating of the weft.

Soumak and leno are two of my favourite weaving techniques; both are very versatile and produce interesting textures.

Soumak

Soumak is a wrapping technique in which the weft thread wraps over one or more warp threads to create a braid-like appearance. It is a very versatile technique and produces different effects based on:
• The direction of wrap.
• Whether it is single, double or more warp threads wrapped together.
• Alternating a soumak row with a row of plain weave.

Leno

Leno is a lace-like technique in which the warp yarns are made to cross each other at certain points. There are many variations of leno:

- Yarns can be crossed right to left or left to right.
- Leno pattern can be used in a small section or over the entire width of the woven fabric.
- Leno can be as simple as a 1/1 or single cross, to a double or 2/2 leno or more.

There is no right or wrong way to weave: the best way is simply to begin!

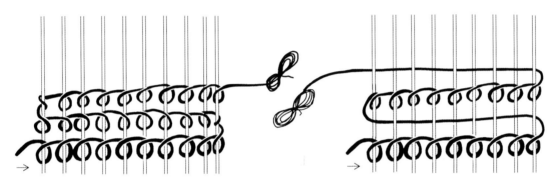

Soumak with the weft thread wrapped over each warp thread.

Alternating rows of soumak and plain weave.

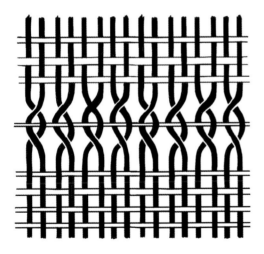

Single cross or 1/1 leno.

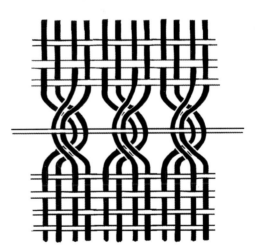

Double cross or 2/2 leno.

RESOURCES

BOOKS

Byrd, Susan J., *A Song of Praise for Shifu* (The Legacy Press, 2014)

Cameron, Julia, *The Artist's Way* (Souvenir Press, 2020)

Fraser, David W., *Ply Split Braided baskets: Exploring Sculpture in Plain Oblique Twining* (Schiffer Publishing, 2014)

Hedges, Julie, *Ply Split Braiding: An Introduction to Designs in Single Course Twining* (Julie Hedges Books, 2006)

King, Heidi, *Peruvian Featherworks: Art of the Precolumbian Era* (Yale University Press, 2012)

Reid, James W., *Magic Feathers: Textile Art from Ancient Peru* (Textile and Art Publications, 2005)

Rowe, Ann Pollard, and Rebecca A.T. Stevens (ed), *Ed Rossbach: 40 years of Exploration and Innovation in Fiber Art* (Lark Books, 1990)

Soroka, Joanne, *Tapestry Weaving: Design and Technique* (The Crowood Press, 2011)

Todd-Hooker, Kathe, with Pat Spark, *So Warped: Warping a Loom for Weaving Tapestry* (Fine Fiber Press & Studios, 2010)

WEBSITES

Sally Pointer
www.youtube.com/c/SallyPointer/featured
YouTube channel for making strings and cordage from plants.

The Marginalian
themarginalian.org
Maria Popova's inspiring search for meaning across literature, science, art and philosophy

MATERIALS

Airedale Yarns (Yarns and tools)
airedaleyarns.co.uk

Handweavers Studio (yarns, books, tools, classes)
handweavers.co.uk

William Hall and Co (yarns)
williamhallyarns.com

The Loom Exchange (weaving tools and books)
theloomexchange.co.uk

WORKSHOPS

Weftfaced
weftfaced.com
Tapestry workshops by Caren Penney, for beginners and advanced students

City Lit
citylit.ac.uk
Brilliant basketry courses under the tutelage of John Page and Polly Pollock for exploring and experimenting with non-loom techniques.

CONTRIBUTORS

Paul Hughes
paulhughesfinearts.com

Doreen Gittens
archipelagotextiles.com

I-Chun Jenkins
fibretheoryart.com

Erroll Pires Nelson
errollsan@yahoo.com

Susan J. Byrd
byrdsnest.net

COLLABORATORS

Camilla Brendon
camillabrendon.com

Vanessa Raw
vanessaraw.co.uk

Vineyard Community
www.vineyardcommunity.org

ACKNOWLEDGEMENTS

I would like to thank Erroll, Susan, Doreen and I-Chun for letting me showcase their inspiring works. It has been a privilege to hear their stories and see their passion for their craft. Many thanks to Paul Hughes for a wonderful lunch, surrounded by beautiful textiles and the photos of Peruvian featherworks. Thanks to Nicola Newman from Batsford for this amazing project. Emily Steadman, a massive thanks for holding my hand from start to finish, for listening patiently to all my rants and for the input and meticulous edits. To Nina Moeller, for filling our studio with positive energy. I would like to thank Yeshen Venema for his calm and reassuring presence and wonderful photography. Thanks to my friends – spread all around the world – for their much valued opinions and encouragement.

Finally, special thanks to my parents and siblings in India for their unconditional love and support. To Rajiv for always being my believing mirror, and to Raima and Piyush, my absolute strength and inspiration.

All photography by Yeshen Venema, except the following: Page 26 (top left and top right) Paul Hughes Fine Arts; 61 Doreen Gittins; 78 and 79 Liam Enderson Photography; 103 (left and centre) Erroll Nelson Pires; 108, 109, 110, 111 Marcus Peel; 112 and 113 Susan Byrd; 11, 25, 31, 44, 45, 55, 56, 58, 60, 66 (left), 94 and 95 the author.

INDEX